PLANET WATCH

Written by
MARTYN BRAMWELL,
DAVID BURNIE, LYNN DICKS,
ROGER FEW

LONDON, NEW YORK, MUNICH,
MELBOURNE, and DELHI

Editors Kitty Blount, Fran Jones, Marek Walisiewicz, Jane Yorke
Editor, this edition Lorrie Mack
Art Editors Janet Allis, Marcus James, Mark Regardsoe
Designer, this edition Lauren Rosier
US Editor Margaret Parrish
Consultants Catriona Lennox, Dr. Philip Whitfield
Consultant, this edition Dr. Lynn Dicks
Jacket Designer Natalie Godwin
Production Editor Siu Chan
Art Director Rachael Foster
Publishing Manager Bridget Giles

Content first published in *Earth Watch, Ocean Watch, Animal Watch,*
and *Food Watch* in the United States, 2001, by DK Publishing. This
revised edition published by DK Publishing in 2009.

375 Hudson Street, New York, New York 10014

09 10 11 12 13 10 9 8 7 6 5 4 3 2 1
PD269 01/09

Copyright © 2001, 2009 Dorling Kindersley Limited

All rights reserved under International and Pan-American Copyright
Conventions. No part of this publication may be reproduced, stored
in a retrieval system, or transmitted in any form or by any means,
electronic, mechanical, photocopying, recording, or otherwise,
without the prior written permission of the copyright owner.
Published in Great Britain by Dorling Kindersley Limited.

A catalog record for this book is available
from the Library of Congress

ISBN 978-0-7566-5820-5

Reproduced by Colourscan, Singapore
Printed and bound by Toppan, China

**Discover more at
www.dk.com**

Contents

Our precious world

Human beings are amazing animals. We can talk to each other, we can plan, and we can change the world around us. We can create art and music, and build things to rival the best that nature has produced. We can make amazing computers. We can see into space and even travel there, and we can understand and alter the workings of our own bodies, and those of other animals and plants. Yet there are some things we aren't so good at.

One is living within our means. We know that our activities are degrading our planet. Other species are going extinct by the thousands because of us. Habitats are being damaged, and the climate itself is changing in a way that will hurt us and many other creatures that share our world. All this is happening because we use more resources than the planet can provide without being harmed.

There are almost seven billion people on Earth, and by the year 2050, there will probably be over nine billion. Already, we have taken about half of the land on Earth for our own use, turning it into crops, forest plantations, pastures, or cities and industrial zones. We are polluting the seas and altering the atmosphere with huge volumes of waste. We are using more than half the accessible fresh water on Earth, and we control the flow of two-thirds of the rivers. We are changing the planet more quickly than we are able to learn about the effects of these changes.

Another thing we are bad at is sharing. While some people are well fed and educated, and have more than enough of what they need, millions of others are dying because they don't have enough food, or clean water. It's an outrage that people are living like this when others are so wealthy.

In lots of countries, children don't learn to read and write or do math like you do. They will never understand science, or read stories, or even learn about the state of the planet. This is an outrage, too.

Modern humans have been on Earth for more than 200,000 years. As a species, we are very young. So what would our school report card say at the start of the 21st century? *"Could try harder. Must share more."*

There is every opportunity for us to reduce our use of resources and share wealth fairly. The first step is learning about our effects on the world. And that, I hope, is why you are reading this book.

Dr. Lynn Dicks

Earth WATCH

As far as we know, the Earth is unique. No other known planet provides the right conditions for life to thrive. And how it thrives here. There are somewhere between 10 and 30 million species of animal, plant, and microbe on Earth, all living together in one huge intricate web of life. One of those species, the human, is changing conditions on Earth significantly at the moment, with its hunger, thirst, and sheer weight of numbers.

People PRESSURE

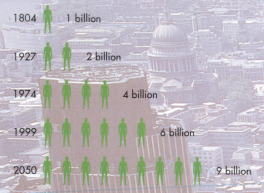

1804	👤	1 billion
1927	👤👤	2 billion
1974	👤👤👤👤	4 billion
1999	👤👤👤👤👤👤	6 billion
2050	👤👤👤👤👤👤👤👤👤	9 billion

Population growth

The world's human population has been growing for thousands of years. But the steepest increase, shown in this chart, has happened in the last 100 years. Today, more than a quarter of a million babies are born every day.

During the last 100 years, something extraordinary has happened to the human race—our numbers have more than tripled. Improvements in hygiene, medicine, and food production are the reasons for this growth. There are now over 6 billion people on the planet, and the total is still growing fast. This steep increase is good news in some ways. It shows that people are healthier than ever before. But the expanding human population also causes problems, because we use up more food, energy, and space every year. Improved family planning is one way in which population growth is now being brought under control.

" Travelers coming to Hong Kong often say that the city is a very wonderful place. However, for me, Hong Kong is a crowded, noisy place. So many people live here—it is hard to find any peace. When I sleep at night, my neighbors are always playing mahjong and their stereo is turned up very loud. In the daytime, construction sites for new homes and office buildings near my school are always making a lot of noise with their machines. Bulldozers tear down walls and move earth, with lots of drillings and hammerings. Although we shut all the windows in our classroom, we can't hear what our teachers say in the lessons. Sometimes, I feel very frustrated about it. "

Virginia Lam

Making space

As the world's population increases, more and more people are moving to cities to find work. It is not easy to make room for all these extra people. In Hong Kong, land has been reclaimed from the sea for office buildings and apartments, and a previously unspoiled coastline has been turned into an international airport.

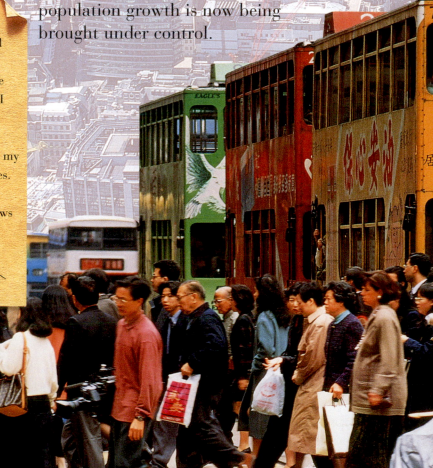

The lure of cities

This shanty town, outside Rio de Janeiro, has been built by people who have moved from the countryside. Their houses do not have running water or proper drainage, and the result is pollution and disease. Scenes like this are common in countries where the population is growing very rapidly.

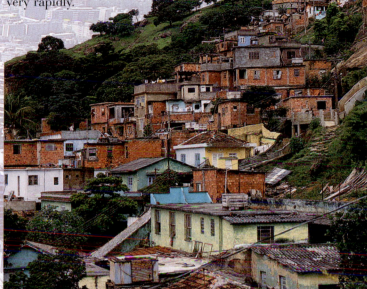

Leaving the countryside

Here an empty farmhouse in France is surrounded by abandoned land. In the 1900s, nine out of 10 people lived in the countryside. Today, less than half the population leads a rural life. Population growth has caused cities to grow and people to move into cities in search of better-paid jobs. In some countries, so many people have moved that not enough remain to farm the land.

> Although the **world's population** is **growing**, the **growth rate** has started **to fall**

People on the move

A highway junction sprawls across the landscape in England. The larger the population, the more people there are traveling. This can mean more cars polluting the atmosphere, and more roads cutting through natural habitats. Using public transportation reduces the pollution, since one vehicle can carry the same number of people as many cars.

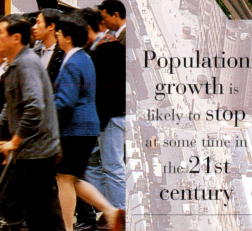

> Population **growth** is likely to **stop** at some time in the **21st** century

The cost of travel

Everyone enjoys going on vacation—particularly to far-flung lands. But air travel has a hidden cost because it is a major source of atmospheric pollution. Air traffic has almost doubled in the last 15 years, and pollution from planes is an increasing problem. Although planes are becoming cleaner and more efficient all the time, their pollution cannot be completely eradicated.

Forest Crisis

Temperate rain forest

These moss-covered trees form part of a unique habitat, the temperate rain forest of the American northwest. Temperate rain forests are found in areas of high rainfall and cool temperatures. These forests once covered a vast area and contained giant coniferous trees many centuries old. Today, most of the original forest has been replaced by planted forest with much less wildlife.

About a third of the **Earth's** original **forests** have been **cut down**

Tropical rain forest

The Amazon River winds through tropical rain forest in Brazil. Tropical rain forests are found in the hot, wet climate zone near the equator. They contain a huge variety of trees, such as mahogany and rosewood, and many other plants—some that scientists have yet to identify. Each tree provides food for many animals, from orangutans to tiny insects.

Forests contain more living creatures and plants than any other land habitat. They are home to more than 10,000 different types of tree, and at least half a million types of animal. But this life is under threat, because forests are being cut down to provide lumber and make way for farms, buildings, and roads. In some parts of the world, including Europe and North America, deforestation started long ago, and now more forests are planted than cut down. But in the tropics, where forest wildlife is richest, large-scale deforestation was at its height in the 1990s, and millions of acres (hectares) are still being cut down every year.

Disappearing trees

This land in Borneo has been stripped of its trees and is crisscrossed by tracks and newly dug terraces. The lumber from tropical rain forests is often very good at resisting decay and is used to make outdoor furniture. Every time people buy products made from this wood, more forest is cleared to keep up the supply.

> ❝Forests do wonderful things. They bind soil to the ground, regulate water supplies, and help govern the climate.❞

UNITED NATIONS DEVELOPMENT PROGRAM: HUMAN DEVELOPMENT REPORT 1998

Sustainable wood

This craftsman is using sustainable wood to make guitars. Sustainable wood is harvested from natural forests or grown on plantations. Young trees are planted when old ones are cut down, so the supply never runs out. Rain-forest ecosystems—the traditional source of wood for musical instruments—can remain unchanged.

ACTION!

Do not buy products made of tropical hardwood unless the wood has been grown in a sustainable way.

Recycle paper—it saves cutting down more trees.

Plants at risk

In tropical rain forests, many plants live high up in trees—their roots clinging to branches. Called epiphytes, they collect moisture from rain and nutrients from dead leaves and dust. When forests are cleared, epiphytes die, as they cannot survive on the ground.

Epiphytic orchid from forest in the Himalayas

People at risk

When forests are cut down, people can be harmed just as much as wildlife. This woman belongs to the Kayan tribe from the Burma-Thailand border—an area where the forest is under threat from logging. Like other people in the tropics, the Kayan rely on the forest for their livelihood. Without it, their traditional way of life ends.

Brazil has formulated **laws** and **regulations** to **reverse** deforestation

FIRE

For millions of years,
forest fires have been a natural feature of the living world. They burn dead wood and leaves, clearing ground for new plants. But when people start fires—on purpose or by accident—the balance is upset. Accidental blazes are very destructive, since they can get out of control, and they happen more often than natural fires, so trees have less time to recover. Also, climate change is increasing the number of fires by bringing drier summers and warmer springs to many places. (Siberian forest fires have increased tenfold in the last 20 years.) But fires started deliberately to clear forests cause the most damage to wildlife, leaving plants and animals homeless.

Forest fire
As flames sweep through a forest, they can destroy trees that may have taken more than 200 years to grow. Birds and large mammals can usually escape the flames, but most small animals are burned alive as the inferno overtakes them. After a major blaze, new saplings soon sprout, but it can take decades for the forest's wildlife to recover fully.

Animals at risk
Southeast Asia's forest fires are very dangerous for orangutans. These endangered apes climb to high branches, but this cannot save them from the flames. Similarly, lemurs living in Madagascar's rain forest have no escape from fire.

Out of the ashes
Fire does not always kill trees because some have defenses against the flames. In fact, certain kinds of pine trees depend on fire, and will not drop their seeds until their cones have been scorched. Forest floor plants burn above ground, but their roots remain safe.

Bulbs are protected under the ground.

Safety underground
Trout lilies can survive fires because they grow from bulbs that are protected from the flames.

Burning bark
Many eucalyptus trees have peeling bark. If the bark catches fire, it falls away without damaging the tree.

ALERT

"Fires ... are one of the greatest ecological disasters of the millennium."

KLAUS TOPFER
HEAD OF UNITED NATIONS
ENVIRONMENT PROGRAM (UNEP)

ACTION!

Do not leave empty bottles on the ground—they can focus the Sun's rays, triggering off a fire.

Never play with fire—a single dropped match can start a blaze.

If you spot a fire, call the fire department immediately.

Putting out the flames
Hovering above the flames, a helicopter uses a "bambi bucket" to drop water on a bush fire. The bucket is refilled by dipping it in a nearby lake.

Animal gains

Attracted by the sight of smoke, this African marabou stork has caught an animal trying to escape from a grassland fire. When a fire burns out, marabous often search the burned grass for the roasted bodies of grasshoppers and lizards.

Feeding
The stork's long beak is not harmed if it touches the hot remains of the fire.

"My name is Sophie Vearing and I live just outside the city of Wagga Wagga in New South Wales, Australia. We have very hot days in the summer and the landscape turns from green to golden brown. The temperature can reach 111°F (44°C) and because there is a very high danger of bush fires, you are not allowed to light fires at all. My stepfather, who is a Group Captain in the Rural Fire Service, is ready to be called to a fire at any time."

Sophie Vearing

Grassland fires

Dry grass catches fire very easily, which is why grasslands, such as these in India, burn more often than forests. Grass fires do not produce much heat, and the grass soon grows again from its roots, because they are kept safe below the ground.

> "Slowing, or even reversing, the existing trend of global warming is the defining challenge of our age."
>
> UN SECRETARY GENERAL
> BAN KI-MOON, 2007

Natural climate change

About 20,000 years ago—near the end of the last Ice Age—much of the northern hemisphere was covered by ice. In the area around New York City, the ice was hundreds of yards (meters) thick. The ice retreated 15,000 years ago, leaving windswept tundra. By about 7,500 years ago, the climate became warmer still, and the tundra turned into forest. These changes were part of a natural cycle that will probably repeat itself—when, no one knows.

Ice Age: 20,000 years ago   Tundra: 15,000 years ago

Changing CLIMATES

Global warming could cause sea levels to rise by **more than 20 in (50 cm)** in the 21st century

Ever since life first appeared on Earth, it has had to cope with changes in climate. Climatologists have several theories about why these natural changes happen, but most of them agree about one thing: our planet is now warming up extremely fast, and this time humans have caused much of the change. The Sun warms the Earth and certain gases, such as carbon dioxide, trap the heat in the atmosphere. This occurs naturally and is called the greenhouse effect. Burning oil, coal, or gas produces extra carbon dioxide, which steps up the greenhouse effect and overheats our planet.

Dry times

People can affect the climate in many ways. In dry places like the Namib Desert, overgrazing by animals strips away the ground's plant cover. Without plants, it is harder for the soil to hold water, and the ground gets hotter in the day. The result is drier air and less rainfall—two things that can turn the land into desert.

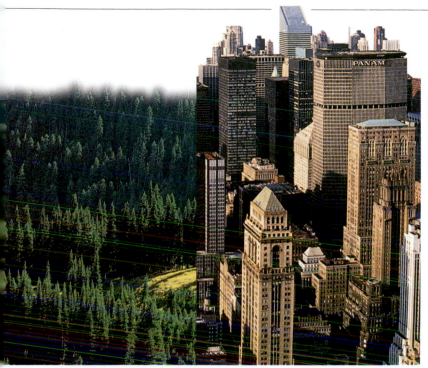

Forest: 7,500 years ago

New York City today

Adapt or die

Natural climate changes usually happen slowly, so plants and animals can adapt. Today's global warming is different because it is happening much more quickly. This rapid warming could wipe out many species that cannot adapt in time.

Gone
The golden toad, from Costa Rica, became extinct in 1989. Scientists believe it was a victim of climate change.

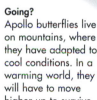

Going?
Apollo butterflies live on mountains, where they have adapted to cool conditions. In a warming world, they will have to move higher up to survive.

Signs of change

In Britain, biologists have discovered that spring is starting earlier each year—almost certainly because of global warming. Some trees now come into leaf 10 days sooner than they did about 40 years ago. Birds are also laying their eggs earlier in the year.

Changing life cycle
Oak buds burst earlier when the weather is unusually warm in the spring. The trees keep their leaves later in warm falls.

Early families
Chaffinches lay their eggs earlier, as spring arrives sooner.

Rising sea levels

A dramatic result of global warming is the melting of the polar icecaps. As temperatures increase, polar glaciers carry more ice from land into the sea. When this ice melts, the sea level rises. Within the next 100 years, low-lying islands such as the Maldives, and coastal cities, are in danger of being engulfed by the sea.

THE GREENHOUSE EFFECT

EXPERIMENT

You will need: 2 small jars, 1 large, clear glass or plastic bowl, some water, and plenty of sunshine!

1 **HALF FILL EACH** jar with water. Put the jars in the sun, either outdoors or indoors next to an open window. Put the clear bowl upside down over one of the jars. Leave for one hour.

Heat trapped inside bowl

2 **REMOVE THE BOWL.** Dip your finger in each jar to compare the temperatures of the water inside. The water in the jar covered by the bowl will be warmer than the water in the other one.

This shows that: the bowl acts like a heat trap, letting light energy in, but preventing infrared (heat) energy from getting out. Carbon dioxide and other gases do something similar in the atmosphere, causing the Earth to warm up.

At the limits

The cool mountain tops in the Cape region of South Africa are home to rare stag beetles. If global warming continues, mountain animals may have to move higher to find the right conditions. But these beetles already live on the summit—they have nowhere to go.

> ❝If enough Arctic ice is lost, polar bears will become extinct.❞
>
> WWF GLOBAL NETWORK

Victims of *change*

ACTION!

Switch off lights when you leave a room.

Reuse plastic carrier bags—making plastic uses lots of energy.

Ask if low-energy lightbulbs can be used at home and at school.

Emperor geese nest on the Yukon Delta in Alaska, one of many wildlife refuges at risk from a rise in sea levels.

The build-up of polluting gases in the atmosphere is slowly changing the weather patterns on Earth and causing global warming. Many wild animals are already feeling the effect of this—some are having to find new homes because they can no longer find the food and the living conditions they need, while others are in danger of disappearing from our Earth altogether.

Threatened refuges

If global warming continues, areas set aside for the protection of wetland birds, such as the emperor goose, may be ruined. Higher temperatures make water expand and melt polar ice, so sea levels rise. Coastal nesting sites of millions of birds may soon be flooded.

Polar bears hunt on ice in the winter and eat little for the rest of the year. Now that the ice is melting earlier, the bears are starting the summer without enough fat stored to keep them healthy.

Moving mosquito
Mosquitoes can spread diseases like malaria when they bite. Cases of malaria in new places suggest that the *Anopheles* mosquito is starting to spread beyond its normal range because of climate change.

Shifting range

As land and sea temperatures rise, many wildlife species will be on the move. Tropical animals may advance into areas that were once too chilly for them. Cold-loving animals will have to move nearer to the poles to find cooler habitats. Some creatures, such as the mosquito, are already extending their habitats to include the new, warm areas.

Lemon sole
Ocean warming may force this fish to start moving to cooler waters. Changes like this could disrupt food chains, causing some species to decline.

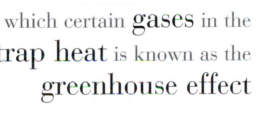

The way in which certain **gases** in the atmosphere **trap heat** is known as the **greenhouse effect**

ANIMAL INSULATION

You will need: 2 identical jam jars with lids, cotton, tape, and warm tap water.

1 **FILL ONE OF THE** jam jars with warm tap water. Put the lid on and cover it all over with a thick layer of cotton, held in place with tape. (The cotton is a substitute for fur.) Fill the other jar with warm tap water. Put the lid on, but leave it uncovered.

You can add food coloring to the water to make the experiment more colorful.

2 **LEAVE THE JARS** for about half an hour, and then dip your finger in both to test the warmth of the water. The water in the covered jar has stayed warm, but the water in the other jar has cooled down.

Heat escapes easily through the uninsulated glass.

This shows that: dense fur keeps warmth in. This is important in a very cold climate but, if the weather warms up, it could make an Arctic animal overheat dangerously.

Warming effects

Polar bears are adapted to cold, Arctic conditions and cannot survive well in warm environments. They already seem to be suffering from climate change, partly because the seals on which they prey have been affected. Ringed seals are having trouble breeding because the snow caves where they rear their pups are melting and collapsing too early in the year.

Some 3 million people are made homeless by floods every year, many of them in coastal zones

FLOOD!

Imagine being swamped by waist-high water, while everything you own is washed away. This happens somewhere in the world almost every week. Floods also destroy crops and increase the risk of disease. Flooding is a natural occurrence and can be useful. For example, in tropical countries such as Bangladesh, monsoon floods spread silt that fertilizes fields. But most floods are harmful, and their effects are getting worse. One reason for this is that more people now live in areas prone to floods. Another is that the world's climate is changing, making floods more severe.

Sinking feeling

Floods are not always caused by rain. In the region around Venice, in northern Italy, floods have gotten worse because a lot of fresh water has been pumped out of the ground. This has made the ground sink, carrying the city with it. At high tide, the sea now floods many of Venice's famous squares, and tourists have to use wooden walkways.

Deadly waters

When Hurricane Katrina hit New Orleans, Louisiana, in 2005, much of its damage was caused by flooding, because the city's defenses failed to protect it. Since then, the defenses have been rebuilt, stronger and higher than ever.

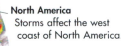

North America
Storms affect the west coast of North America.

South America
During an El Niño year, the sea off South America gets warmer.

El Niño rain
Ecuador and Peru receive more rain than normal.

El Niño

Every few years, a strong, warm current called El Niño (the Christ Child) arrives in December off the coast of Peru. Caused when warm water and moist air fail to blow west across the Pacific as usual, it brings heavy rain to the Peruvian deserts, and drought to Australia and Indonesia. Recently, El Niño has been arriving more often, and lasting longer.

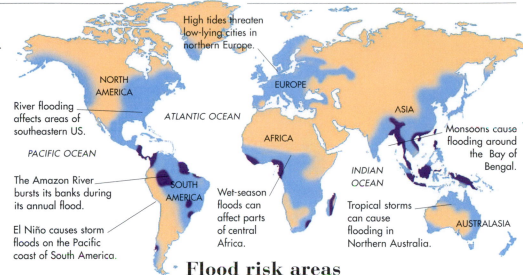

High tides threaten low-lying cities in northern Europe.

River flooding affects areas of southeastern US.

The Amazon River bursts its banks during its annual flood.

El Niño causes storm floods on the Pacific coast of South America.

Monsoons cause flooding around the Bay of Bengal.

Wet-season floods can affect parts of central Africa.

Tropical storms can cause flooding in Northern Australia.

NORTH AMERICA
ATLANTIC OCEAN
PACIFIC OCEAN
SOUTH AMERICA
EUROPE
AFRICA
ASIA
INDIAN OCEAN
AUSTRALASIA

Annual Rainfall

- More than 78 in (2,000 mm)
- 20–78 in (500–2,000 mm)
- Less than 20 in (500 mm)

Flood risk areas

Your chances of being hit by a flood depend on where you live. This world map shows annual rainfall. In the tropics, monsoon rain and tropical storms cause floods. In other parts of the world, heavy rain makes rivers burst their banks and floods occur. Earthquakes can also produce flooding because they trigger off tidal waves.

Between 1986 and 1995, **floods** were responsible for more than **half** of all **fatalities** caused by natural catastrophes

Burst banks

Working against the clock, these people are building an artificial bank to hold back the Missouri River. Permanent artificial banks can prevent floods in normal years, but they can make flood water pile up after very heavy rain. If a bank breaks, this pent-up water suddenly pours onto the land, with disastrous results.

Global warming causes more storms and heavier rains, and increases flooding

The amount of **energy** used by the **human race** has almost **doubled** in **30 years**

Filthy

Nuclear energy

Uranium fuel is lowered into the core of a nuclear reactor. Unlike power plants that burn fossil fuels, nuclear reactors don't produce waste gases, so they don't pollute the air. However, uranium is a hazardous substance because it emits lethal radiation. Even after the fuel has been used, the radiation takes tens of thousands of years to fade away.

On average, **every person** on Earth **uses** the equivalent of **1.9 tons** of **oil** a **year**

Every switch you flick is a reminder that modern life depends on energy. We use huge amounts of energy. Most of it comes from burning fossil fuels, such as oil, coal, and gas, which are cheap and convenient. But fossil fuels create pollution when they are moved around, and even more when they are burned. Scientists are finding ways of reducing pollution by using fossil fuels more efficiently. We can prevent it entirely if we use clean energy, such as solar, wind, and water power.

Gas on tap

Inching its way across the ground, this crane is laying a natural gas pipeline in Siberia. This kind of work can damage natural habitats, and it also opens up wilderness areas that used to be difficult for people to reach. However, natural gas does have one advantage—it contains very little sulfur, which makes it the cleanest burning fossil fuel.

Mining coal

Huge amounts of rock have been cut away to reach the coal hidden below the ground in this Australian mine. Extracting coal is dangerous, and it also destroys natural habitats. When coal near the surface is dug up, trees and other plants are bulldozed away.

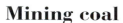

FUEL

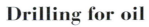

About **90** percent of the world's **crude oil** has **already** been **located**

ACTION!

Switch off your computer when you are not using it.

In winter, put on more clothes before you turn up the heat.

Don't leave your television set on standby.

Drilling for oil

This pump is extracting oil from beneath the ground. At one time, oil was always drilled on land, but over the years, many land-based oil wells have run dry. Today, a large amount of the oil we use comes from wells drilled into the seabed. Oil pollutes the seabed by seeping out of wells, and it also kills coastal wildlife when tankers run aground.

Most of the energy used by the computer turns into waste heat.

Generating electricity

Power plants generate the electricity we use at home, at school, and at work. Coal-fired power plants and their cooling towers, shown below, produce air pollution and waste heat. Modern gas-fired power plants are more efficient and also less polluting.

Using electricity

When you use a computer, you may find it hard to believe that you are polluting the environment. Switching on a lamp, using the telephone, or turning on a fan could all have the same effect. All these appliances need electricity. This almost certainly comes from a power plant that burns coal, gas, or oil, or from one that uses nuclear fuels.

When **fossil fuels** are **burned** to produce electricity, over **half** their **energy** is **lost** in **waste**

Clean air... Dirty air

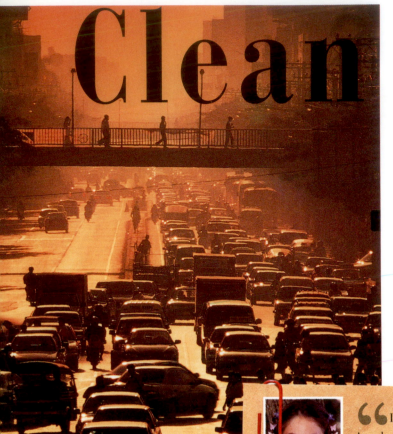

T here is nothing new about dirty air. In the past, when most homes had coal fires, city air was so sooty that it caused thick, dense fogs—in London, England, they were called "pea soupers." Today, there are fewer home fires, but we have other sources of air pollution. They include products that release airborne chemicals, and household garbage that gives off toxic substances when it's burned. But the most significant sources of dirty air are fossil fuels such as coal, oil, and natural gas. They are burned by power plants, and by cars, trucks, buses, and planes.

City smog

Bangkok, Thailand, on a sunny day is covered in yellow smog. This modern smog is a serious problem in cities with a warm climate. Smog is produced when gases from car exhausts react with sunlight. The result is a choking brown haze that contains nitrogen oxides, ozone, and other poisonous gases. Many cities have smog alerts when conditions are very bad.

Fuel from sugar cane
The sap is extracted from sugar cane and fermented to turn the sugar into ethanol.

" I live in Los Angeles, California, and there is a lot of smog here sometimes. Smog is a type of pollution that you can't get away from. It's full of chemicals and dust, junk, and yucky stuff. When it gets in your lungs you can only breathe for about a second, and you feel like you're going to keep coughing for the rest of your life. When you run, it's even harder because then you really feel like you can't breathe at all. Since I have asthma, my lungs are a bit more sensitive than most people's, so I really feel the difference when there's a smog alert.

Sophia Leikin

Low-pollution future

Cars can run on plant fuels such as bioethanol, which comes from sugary crops like sugar cane. Because plants absorb carbon dioxide as they grow, burning these does not add extra carbon dioxide to the atmosphere. But it still pollutes the air in cities.

Clean run
Electric cars produce no exhaust fumes, and if they use renewable electricity, they produce no harmful emissions either.

Acid rain

When coal and oil are burned, they release sulfur dioxide, a highly acidic gas that produces acid rain, which makes trees sicken and die. It also harms wildlife in lakes and rivers, and eats into stone buildings. Modern power plants have cleaning systems that remove sulfur dioxide from their smoke. Cars don't have these, but in many countries the law regulates the sulfur content of car fuels.

Acid attack
This ancient statue has lost its head and arms. The culprit is acid rain, which has slowly weakened the stone.

Dying trees
Acid rain has changed the chemistry of the soil and damaged these spruce trees. They are suffering from dieback, which is when the young shoots die.

ACID RAIN

EXPERIMENT

You will need: 2 small jars, tap water, some vinegar, and 2 pieces of chalk.

1 **POUR WATER** into one jar until it is a third full. Pour vinegar into the other jar until it is also a third full. Drop one piece of chalk into each jar. Leave overnight.

2 **LOOK AT THE JARS** the next day. The chalk in the vinegar has been eaten away and partially dissolved. The chalk in the water is still whole.

This shows that: although it is a weak acid, vinegar can dissolve chalk. Acid rain eats into chalk and limestone in just the same way.

In cold places, **winter air** pollution produces **acid snow** that can taste as **sour** as a **lemon**

The **damage** to the **ozone layer** caused by **CFCs** will not be fully repaired until **2050** at the earliest

Ozone rescue

At ground level, ozone gas is dangerous. But high up above the ground, it forms a natural shield that protects us from the Sun's ultraviolet light. In recent years, this layer has been eaten away by CFCs, which are chemicals once used in aerosols, refrigerators, and plastic packaging. In 1987, an international agreement came into force to phase out CFCs.

Today's aerosols are CFC-free

Aerosol can
CFCs, sprayed from aerosol cans like this one, take more than 100 years to go away.

CFCs can leak from fridges that are thrown away.

Perils of POLLUTION

Day after day, chemicals flush into rivers, gases seep into the air, and waste is strewn on the land. The planet is being contaminated for all living things. Pollution is often invisible, but it can do as much damage to habitats as flames and bulldozers. Pollution weakens animals by poisoning their food supplies. Some poisons, or toxins, build up in animals' bodies until they reach dangerous levels. For species already suffering from habitat disruption, pollution of their remaining home can be devastating. Some people are now finding alternatives to chemical pesticides, and using energy from sources that do not produce harmful waste, such as solar and wind power.

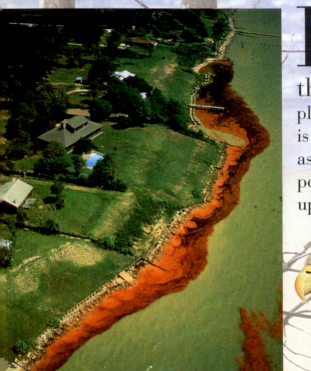

Deadly damage

After an oil spill at sea, oil washes up onto beaches, as here in Texas. Oil can cause problems for wildlife before it is cleared up, killing many seabirds and sand-dwelling creatures. The oil clogs up feathers and fur, and poisons animals if it enters their bodies.

Chemical contamination

Top predators, such as the bald eagle of North America, suffer when their prey is contaminated with toxins. Pollution is not always an accident. Some factories release chemicals into the air and rivers, and farmers' pesticides can poison wildlife on land and in the water. Since the pesticide DDT was banned in North America, bald eagle populations are recovering.

Failed eggs

These sparrowhawk eggs were too fragile to develop because of harmful pesticides consumed by the parent birds. Today, pesticides are often made from plant extracts, and are kinder to the environment than those based on artificial chemicals.

Dangerous dinner
Eating plants contaminated by radiation can cause birth defects in animals.

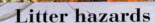

Radiation

Pastures of wild caribou and farm animals were contaminated after a nuclear accident at the Chernobyl power plant in Ukraine in 1986. Caribou in Lapland ate contaminated moss, and many had to be slaughtered. Severe radioactive pollution is rare, but its effects on animals can be disastrous.

Litter hazards

Organized clean-up projects make places like this Alaska beach look better, and also remove hazards for wildlife. Litter, such as discarded fishing nets, lead weights, plastic bags, and plastic yokes that hold drink cans, can entangle, poison, and choke wild animals.

Fighting pollution

Environmental groups such as Greenpeace campaign to stop people from polluting the environment. In 1996, members of Greenpeace protested about the Brent Spar oil platform, which was going to be dumped on the ocean bed. They claimed that the structure was full of toxic materials. The protest helped to change disposal plans for all oil and gas rigs in the area.

LONG-TERM LITTER

EXPERIMENT

You will need: 2 empty jam jars, damp soil collected from outside, a thin slice of apple, a square of aluminum foil, a small piece of plastic carrier bag, a large sheet of paper.

1 HALF FILL THE jam jars with soil. Put the slice of apple in one, and the square of foil and piece of plastic bag in the other. Cover them over with soil and leave the jars in a warm place.

Substances like foil and plastic may take hundreds of years to decompose.

2 AFTER A WEEK, empty the contents of both jars onto the paper. You will see that the apple has begun to shrivel up and decay, but the foil and the plastic look like new.

This shows that: tiny organisms in soil break down natural waste, but litter made from metal and plastic does not decompose easily. It can stay in the environment for a long time, harming generations of wildlife.

Wasteful

Fatal attraction

For wild animals, our household waste can be life-threatening. Attracted by the smell of rotting food, this bear is exploring a garbage dump. It risks being injured by broken glass, or choking on discarded plastic.

Plastic is often **recyclable**, even though **most** of it gets **thrown away**

Toxic time bomb

Industrial waste can be difficult to deal with because it is often poisonous. These chemical drums have broken open, which makes the problem even more serious. Because waste like this is expensive to dispose of safely, it is often dumped illegally.

In nature, there is no such thing as waste, because the material that living things produce gets broken down and reused. But in the human world, it is very different. Every year, each one of us produces up to three-quarters of a ton of household waste, adding to a growing mountain of garbage that has to find a home. But many of the items that we throw away are actually resources in disguise. Paper, glass, and metal can be recycled and reused, while kitchen and garden waste can be turned into compost that improves the fertility of the soil.

We need to **think** about ways to **reduce** the amount of **waste** we create

Indecent burial

Surrounded by a garbage-strewn landscape, this bulldozer is spreading out household waste. When the site is full, the waste will be covered with soil, but it will have to be monitored for years to come. This is because waste produces inflammable gases and polluting sludge as it breaks down.

World

Compost from waste

At this processing plant in France, organic matter from household waste is being turned into compost that can be spread on fields. Organic matter makes up nearly a quarter of household garbage. It includes anything that comes from plants or animals, such as vegetable peelings and other leftover food.

Dutch treatment

These recycling bins in the Netherlands have been color-coded according to their use—blue for paper, orange for textiles, green for glass, and yellow for cans. This speeds up the system of recycling and makes the whole process more energy efficient.

Paper can only be **recycled** up to 8 times before the fibers are **destroyed**

Longer life

Household waste includes many different materials that can be recycled. Glass, for example, can be recycled forever because it never breaks down. Metal, as used for drink cans, can also be recycled indefinitely.

All sorts of bottles, cans, and papers are suitable for recycling.

ACTION!

Separate out your waste and recycle whatever you can.

Take your lunch in a sandwich box rather than wrapping it in foil.

Use and refill your own water bottle.

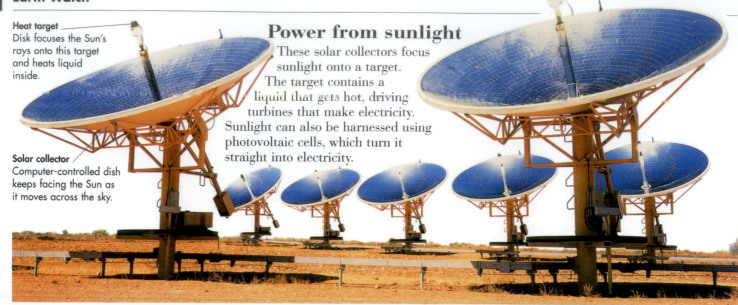

Heat target
Disk focuses the Sun's rays onto this target and heats liquid inside.

Power from sunlight

These solar collectors focus sunlight onto a target. The target contains a liquid that gets hot, driving turbines that make electricity. Sunlight can also be harnessed using photovoltaic cells, which turn it straight into electricity.

Solar collector
Computer-controlled dish keeps facing the Sun as it moves across the sky.

A Cleaner Future

In a single day, enough solar energy falls on Earth to keep the human race going for more than 15 years. Unlike energy from fossil or nuclear fuels, this energy is self-renewing, and it causes no pollution. It keeps the planet warm, and it drives the currents that keep wind and water on the move. Today, only a tiny fraction of this energy is harnessed for human needs, mainly because it is too expensive. But technology is improving, and clean energy is becoming cheaper. Using clean energy could solve many of the world's pollution problems.

Powerful winds

One day, wind turbines might generate enough electricity to provide much of our power. Although some people think they're noisy and spoil the view, they produce no pollution. Also, they can be erected at sea, where it's very windy.

Screens keep the house cool in summer.

Solar-powered lighting

The energy-efficient house

This house in Vienna, Austria, has been specially designed to use energy as efficiently as possible. Its windows let in lots of sunshine during the winter, but they keep most of it out in summer. The walls are well insulated so the temperature inside remains steady. Its hot-water supply is heated partly by solar power.

Water power

Close to one-sixth of all the electricity used in the world is generated by water. The water, held back by dams like this one in Sri Lanka, is piped downhill to drive turbines. This is called hydroelectric power.

Dead end

Hydroelectric power is clean, but it can cause problems for water wildlife. Sockeye salmon, which migrate up rivers to breed, have been harmed by hydroelectric programs because large dams stop them from reaching the places where they lay their eggs.

Insulated walls prevent heat inside the house from escaping.

South-facing windows let sunshine in during the winter.

In theory, **wind** and **wave** power **could** generate **all** the **energy** that we **need**

Energy from the Earth

At this power plant in New Zealand, steam from hot rocks is used to drive turbines, producing pollution-free power. This clean source of power is known as geothermal energy. It uses heat from the interior of the Earth in places where this natural heat is not far below the surface.

In **Iceland**, four-fifths of the country's **homes** are **kept warm** by **geothermal** energy

---

WATERWHEEL

EXPERIMENT

You will need: 2 thin plastic plates, modeling clay, plastic can lids, double-sided tape, pencil, water, and sink.

1 PLACE ONE PLATE over a piece of modeling clay. Using a pencil, make a hole at the exact center, pushing the point into the modeling clay. Repeat with the second plate.

2 USING THE TAPE, stick the lids to the edge of one plate at six evenly spaced points. The lids should circle the plate, each one facing the bottom of the one in front.

3 TAKE THE second plate and, using the tape, stick it to the lids so it sits opposite the other plate. The lids are "sandwiched" between the two plates.

4 PUSH THE pencil through the holes in the plates. The waterwheel is complete. Hold it over a sink and let water run onto it from a faucet. As the water fills each lid, the wheel turns.

This shows that: by using a waterwheel, the energy in moving water can be converted into energy that can do useful work.

Water WATCH

Every creature on Earth needs water in order to live. Most of the water is in the oceans, where it is home to a huge range of plants and animals. On land, clean, fresh water is becoming a dangerously scarce resource, as billions of people use more and more of it all the time.

PRECIOUS

Water is essential for life. In some parts of the world, fresh water is easy to find, but in others it's hidden underground. Water moves in a continuous cycle. It falls to Earth as rain or snow and makes its way to the oceans, either above or below ground. Every day the Sun's heat evaporates billions of tons of water from the oceans. Water vapor in the air forms clouds and falls again as fresh rainwater. At one time, humans had little effect on this cycle, but in the past 100 years, this has changed. We now use half of all the freshwater in rivers, lakes, and streams around the world. In some places, supplies are running out.

> **"Human demands are about to collide with the ability of the hydrological cycle to supply water."**
>
> FOOD AND AGRICULTURE ORGANIZATION

Surface water

Tumbling down a rocky hillside in Oregon, water races toward its meeting with the sea. This is surface water—water that is found above the ground. Surface water includes ice sheets, rivers, and lakes. Water is vital to all living things because they need it for essential processes such as feeding and breathing.

RESOURCE

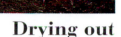

Long beak can reach insects, snails, and small frogs.

Brown plumage helps the bird camouflage itself among the reeds.

Long widely splayed toes prevent the bird from sinking into soft ground.

Drying out

Many birds, such as this water rail, live in freshwater wetlands and depend on them to survive. Sometimes the water is diverted or drained away to make new land for houses or farms. When this happens, wetland birds are forced out. Because they cannot adapt to other habitats, their numbers decrease.

Underground water

In some desert regions, the only place you can find water is below the ground. These women are drawing water from a well in Mali, on the edge of the Sahara Desert. The water first falls as rain. It trickles through the rocks and collects in natural reservoirs deep under the ground.

United States
656,000 gallons
(2,483,000 liters)

Australia
368,000 gallons
(1,393,000 liters)

United Kingdom
329,000 gallons
(1,245,000 liters)

Kenya
189,000 gallons
(714,000 liters)

One year's water

Some countries use far more water than others. The amount one person uses in a year is shown above. The figures include water used for drinking and washing, as well as in industry and farming. Making just one cotton shirt uses 713 gallons (2,700 liters). That's enough drinking water to last you for nearly three years.

ACTION!

Put a brick in your toilet cistern—when you flush, less water is used.

Take a shower instead of a bath.

Use a bowl of water for washing instead of a running faucet.

NATURAL WATER FILTER

EXPERIMENT

You will need: scissors, plastic bottle, compass, large plate, protective gloves, spoon, pebbles, gravel, small stones, coarse sand, fine sand, pitcher, water, soil.

1 USING THE scissors, cut the top off the bottle. With the compass, carefully pierce about six small holes around the side of the bottle, near the base.

Pierce holes with point of compass

2 STAND THE BOTTLE on the plate. Put on the gloves. Spoon in the pebbles, then the gravel, followed by the small stones. Spoon in the coarse sand and then the fine sand.

Soil collects as water is filtered

3 PUT A HANDFUL of soil into a pitcher half-full of water. Stir it thoroughly, and then pour the mixture into the open top of the bottle. The water that collects on the plate will be much cleaner than the water in the pitcher.

Small stones

Coarse sand

Fine sand

This shows that: water is naturally filtered as it flows through the ground.

WATER

People in many parts of the world are desperately short of water, and the problem is getting worse. Wasteful use of water and poorly planned crop watering (irrigation) programs are having a devastating effect on communities and the environments they depend on. People need clean, fresh water to drink. They need water for sanitation, and for their crops and livestock. Droughts cannot be prevented, but even small amounts of rainfall can go a long way if they are carefully collected and stored.

Precious resource

For many people living in West Africa, the only place to collect fresh drinking water is from the village well—where it is pumped from deep underground. The water in open wells and surface streams is often polluted by animal and human waste. Thanks to international aid, many wells are drilled to provide communities with clean, healthy water.

> **"Nearly one billion people today lack safe sources of drinking water."**
>
> UNITED NATIONS, 2008

Vanished livelihoods
Aral Sea fishing boats lie stranded due to a failed irrigation program.

Asia's dying lake

The Aral Sea in western Asia was one of the world's largest lakes. But large-scale desert irrigation projects built by Russia in the 1960s diverted the rivers that used to feed it. Today, the lake has lost five-sixths of its water. The surrounding farmland has returned to desert. Salt flats cover the dried-up lake bed, and the local fisheries have been ruined.

CRISIS

Poisoned land

For more than 30 years, hundreds of millions of gallons of water have been drawn from Pakistan's Indus River to feed farm irrigation programs. Now an ecological disaster threatens. Much of the farmland has been turned into infertile salt flats. These are formed when mineral salts in the soil are drawn up to the surface as water evaporates. This rock-hard layer is toxic to plants and too hard to plow.

Rainfall harvesting techniques in **the dry** regions of **India** have **revived** the Arvari River

Saving water

New cultivation methods, such as hydroponics, allow farmers to feed and water their greenhouse crops with much less waste. Tomato plants are grown without soil in bags filled with gravel. Just the right amounts of water containing nutrients can be pumped through the gravel directly to the plant roots.

Rainfall harvesting

Low earth- or stone-wall dams, called johads, are built on sloping farmland in India. They hold back precious rainwater and help it soak into the ground. Crops can draw on the stored water even through dry periods.

SALT FLAT FORMATION

EXPERIMENT

You will need: clean plastic dish or take-out food tray, table salt, soil, rubber gloves, pitcher of water, magnifying glass.

1 **PLACE ABOUT** ½ in (1 cm) of salt in the dish and cover with 2 in (5 cm) of soil. Press the soil down firmly.

2 **WATER THE SOIL** until it is wet through. Leave the dish on a warm, sunny windowsill. When the soil dries out, water it again. Repeat this process for two weeks.

3 **CHECK THE SOIL** surface with a magnifying glass each day. After a few days, tiny salt crystals will appear. After two weeks, the whole surface of the soil will be covered in a hard, salty crust.

This shows that: irrigation water can dissolve salts in the ground, draw them to the surface, and leave them there as the water evaporates.

Always wash your hands after handling soil.

Crop circles

The crops in these fields in Oregon are grown in circles to suit the irrigation method used by the farmer. When rainfall is scarce, a long water pipe, supported by sets of wheels with soft tires to protect the soil, trundles around a central point and sprays the crop as it goes.

Evils of Pollution

Once water is used, it does not simply disappear. Sooner or later it finds its way back into nature's water cycle, which eventually takes it to the sea. But used water is often polluted with waste from factories, farms, and homes. Some of this waste can harm animals and plants that live in water, while other waste causes disease. In the world's richest countries, water pollution has been a problem for a long time, although now tighter regulations are reducing the damage. But in many poorer countries, pollution is increasing, and clean water can be hard to find.

Chemical waste

One look at this stream shows that its water is unsafe to drink, or even to touch. But polluted water is not always this easy to spot. Some waste chemicals dissolve without leaving any visible traces, which makes them difficult to control.

Gas from this cylinder is burned to speed up the process of extracting gold.

Miner wears no protective gloves and can get skin poisoning from the mercury.

Mercury in the Amazon

This Brazilian miner is extracting gold by mixing it with mercury. Once the gold has been purified, the mercury is often dumped in rivers. Mercury kills freshwater wildlife and can poison people if it gets into drinking water.

Oil on shore

Volunteers are cleaning up oil that has been washed onto a beach in Wales. Oil spills like this can be deadly to sea birds. The oil clogs up feathers, making it impossible for the bird to fly and hard for it to stay warm.

A bird may swallow oil when preening its feathers.

Oil can be removed with dishwashing liquid.

Some rivers in the world are so polluted with industrial and agricultural waste that they are said to be biologically dead

In hot water

Oil refineries and power plants often use cold water to get rid of unwanted heat. The water, which becomes hot, is poured into rivers like this one. Heat reduces the amount of oxygen that the river water can hold, which can cause fish to die.

ACTION!

If you see signs of pollution, such as oil on beaches, inform the local authorities.

Do not drop litter into rivers, into the sea, or onto beaches.

Take unused paint to your local recycling center.

Each algal strand is thinner than a hair.

When millions of these strands cover the water, the result is called "algal bloom."

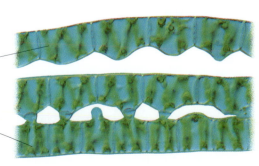

Going for growth

Microscopic algae like these grow in rivers, lakes, and ponds, and normally cause no harm. But if fertilizer or sewage pollutes the water, they grow much faster. The algae use up oxygen when they die and rot away, leaving little for the other water wildlife.

Perfect BALANCE

Phytoplankton
These tiny plants drift near the sea's surface. They use the Sun's energy to convert water and carbon dioxide into food.

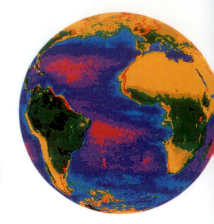

Plants and animals that live in the sea look very different from those on land. But their ways of life and habitats are similar. Plants within the oceans do the same job as the grasslands and forests on land—they capture the Sun's energy and turn it into food. As on land, these plants provide food for grazing animals, while the grazers, in turn, provide food for the hunters. Marine habitats range from rocky and sandy shores through coral reefs and seaweed forests to the cold, dark depths of ocean basins. Communities of plants and animals have evolved to meet the challenges of each habitat. Disturbing this balance can have far-reaching effects for both animal and human life.

Ocean pastures
This satellite picture has been colored to show the distribution of phytoplankton in the oceans. Red areas have the most, blue the least. These plants provide food for marine animals, and release oxygen into the atmosphere.

Zooplankton
The smallest animals in the food chain include the microscopic larvae of crabs, shrimp, and other creatures.

Airborne predator
Many seabirds, such as this brown pelican, feed almost entirely on small fish.

First predators
Schools of small fish, such as these anchovies, are the first of a series of predators (animals that prey on other animals).

Food chain
Every living thing needs food to fuel the processes of life—growth, development, and reproduction. A food chain is a line of feeding links between one type of creature and another. In the sunlit zones, phytoplankton grow and multiply. These tiny plants are eaten by animal plankton. Fish, such as anchovies, eat these but are eaten, in turn, by still larger fish. This continues until there is a top predator, such as a shark. A food chain need not be long. Some whales feed directly on plankton.

A drop of **sea** water can contain **millions** of **phytoplankton**

Fish hunters
Larger fish, such as cod, feed on the smaller fish as well as on clams, shrimp, and worms.

Squid fishing off the US coast leaves seals and dolphins short of food

Upsetting the balance

Human activities can have a disastrous effect when they upset the balance of hunters and hunted in the oceans. Fishing for sharks is a popular sport off Tasmania. Sharks feed on octopuses, and removing the sharks causes the number of octopuses to rise. Octopuses then eat more of their natural prey—spiny lobsters—and the balance is changed.

Octopus
The octopus has a powerful beak, which makes short work of lobsters, snails, and shellfish.

Large sharks have only one natural enemy—humans

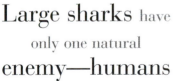

Top predator
This great white shark is at the top of the food chain. It can only be killed by humans, old age, or disease.

ADAPTING TO HABITAT
EXPERIMENT

You will need: rubber gloves, 2 types of seaweed, 2 zip-lock bags, colored tape, kitchen scales, clothes pins and line.

Color-code the seaweeds.

Store in a zip-lock bag.

1 WHEN YOU VISIT A ROCKY BEACH collect two small bunches of seaweed. One of the seaweeds should grow at the water's edge at low tide. The other should be gathered from near the high tide mark.

Weigh out an equal amount of each seaweed.

2 CAREFULLY WEIGH each bunch of seaweed. Remove pieces from the heavier bunch until it weighs exactly the same as the lighter bunch of seaweed.

3 HANG THE bunches out in a dry place. Weigh them daily for four days. The seaweed that grew near the water will lose weight faster than the one that grew higher up the beach.

This shows that: seaweeds that grow higher up the beach—and are out of the sea for most of the day—are better adapted for holding on to vital water.

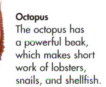

Reef in DANGER

Two-thirds of reefs in the Caribbean are threatened by overharvesting and pollution

Coral reefs are the richest habitats in the ocean. Just a few miles (kilometers) of reef can contain well over 3,000 species—from minute shrimp to fish weighing more than half a ton. A reef is a massive, rocky structure but it is also surprisingly fragile. The tiny animals, called polyps, which build the reef can only thrive when conditions are just right. The water must be shallow enough for sunlight to reach the coral, and the water should be at least 65°F (18°C) warm. It must also be free from mud and pollution. Any change in these conditions puts the reef at risk.

The living reef

A coral reef swarms with life. With all its nooks and crannies it provides a home for hundreds of different types of marine plants and animals as well as the living corals themselves. The reef is a complete ecosystem in its own right—a complex world where scavengers, filter-feeders, plant-eaters, and hunters all depend on one another for survival.

Tentacles are armed with stinging cells.

There is just one body opening.

Each polyp makes its own skeleton cup.

Only the surface of the reef is alive.

Reef builders

A reef is built from the piled-up skeletons of tiny animals called polyps. Each polyp makes a hard limestone cup to live in— poking out its tentacles to feed, and pulling back inside when danger comes along. When the polyps die, their skeletons remain. These gradually build up to create a coral reef.

The reef builds up layer by layer.

Brain coral

Organ-pipe coral

Staghorn coral

A market for coral

Corals grow in a range of appealing shapes and colors, and thousands of tons are sold every year to tourists. This Bali islander is collecting a basket of dead coral to sell. Each time a lump of coral is sold, another piece is hacked off a reef to take its place on the market stall. It can take decades for the coral to regrow.

Mining reefs for building **materials** continues in the **Indian Ocean**

> "Coral reefs are home to plant and animal species found nowhere else on Earth. They have been called the rain forests of the sea."
>
> WORLD RESOURCES INSTITUTE 2008

Some of the world's coral reefs may be **2.5 million years old**

Bleached coral

Corals' color comes from tiny algae inside them. If water temperature rises, or the reef is polluted, the algae leave and the coral turns white (see above). If the right conditions don't return quickly, the reef dies. A rise of 1.8°F (1°C) can trigger a bleaching event. Experts have predicted that, because of climate change, this could be happening every year by 2020.

Anchor damage

Reefs suffer a great deal of damage when tourist boats lower anchors and chains to the seafloor (shown here). Although the old limestone rock at the heart of a reef is tough enough to rip the bottom out of a ship, the thin layer of living coral on the surface of the reef is delicate.

ACTION!

If you are diving or snorkeling on a reef, look—but never touch.

Do not buy souvenirs made of coral, rare shells, or parts of other reef creatures.

COASTAL *Care*

At the boundary between land and sea, the coasts provide a huge variety of habitats for some of the most fascinating animals and plants on our planet. But coasts also attract people in vast numbers—many come on vacation, others to find permanent homes. This increases the level of development and pollution in these areas. However, worldwide beach clean-up events are helping to preserve the world's coastlines. The projects help people to understand the problems and enable them to do something positive.

Cliff tops
Short grasses grow in the thin soil. Puffins and Manx shearwaters nest in cliff-top burrows.

Rockpools
Home to crabs, limpets, anemones, and starfish, the rock pools are filled with many seaweeds.

Sandy beach
Hundreds of species of worms and shellfish live hidden in their burrows beneath the sand.

Rocky headlands
Birds such as kittiwakes, guillemots, and razorbills nest on narrow cliff ledges.

Survival techniques

The coast is a harsh place. Seaside plants must cope with salt spray—and must also survive on shifting sands, or tiny amounts of soil in rock crevices. Many have short stems and cushion-like leaves to protect them from the buffeting and drying effect of the wind. To avoid the sun and marauding seabirds, worms and cockles burrow into the sand when the tide goes out, while limpets clamp themselves to the rocks and crabs hide under fronds of damp seaweed.

Marram dunes

The shifting surface of a sand dune is a difficult place for any plant to take root. However, marram grass grows quickly and has roots that spread sideways as well as down. This helps to anchor the sand and allows other plants to get established.

Dense roots bind loose sand grains together.

I live in New Jersey, right near Atlantic City. The beach here has changed a lot over the years. When my parents were kids it was clean, but now the water pollution is so bad that fish often wash up dead. If you walk along the beach, you find broken bottles, plastic cups, and even cigarette butts. Because I care about the beach, I do voluntary work with a group called Clean Ocean Action who try to protect the ocean. This makes the beach a better place for the animals that live there—and for the people, too.

ACTION!

Shred or cut through plastic six-pack yokes before throwing them away.

Find out how you can take part in a local beach-cleaning project—or one that's near your favorite vacation spot.

Beach clean-up

In many countries, young people take part in beach clean-up operations. The detailed surveys carried out during these events show what the main types of garbage are and where they come from. This helps governments make better enviromental laws.

Lethal litter

The most dangerous items of litter are plastic bags and yokes that hold drink cans. Turtles often mistake bags for their main food—jellyfish—and choke on them. Birds and even young seals get their heads or legs caught in plastic yokes.

This American coot is caught in the plastic loops of a six-pack yoke.

Seabird sanctuary

The eggs and nestlings of some species, like these little terns, are often well camouflaged. This means they are almost impossible to see against a background of pebbles—until it's too late. Look out for notices that ask you to keep off beaches where birds are breeding.

Chemical beach

Occasionally, a metal drum, or a plastic container of liquid or powder, may wash up on a beach. It could contain acid or poisonous chemicals—and might even be giving off dangerous fumes. This is no ordinary beach garbage and should not be approached. Tell a parent or teacher.

EXPLOITING
the SEA

The oceans have always provided people with food. Today, there are other important industries that rely on raw materials from the sea. Oil and gas are extracted from rocks beneath the ocean floor, and tin and titanium are dredged from coastal sand bars. Certain seaweeds are gathered and used in processed foods, while seawater itself is treated to make clean drinking water as well as salt. The deep ocean floors are littered with fist-sized nodules rich in manganese, copper, and nickel. They are not exploited yet—but they could prove important mineral resources of the future.

Fish farming

In many countries, fish are reared in wire-mesh pens. Although fish farming reduces the numbers of fish caught in the wild, it does have problems. Here, fish food has caused a blanket of algae to grow near the pens. This algae can choke natural life nearby.

Energy from the sea

Almost a quarter of the oil and gas we use comes from beneath the shallow seas of the continental shelves. The oil and gas are extracted by drilling down through the rocks from huge platforms, such as this one in the North Sea. Oil platform workers check constantly for leaks and spills that could harm the environment.

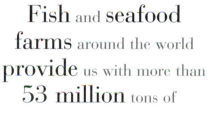

Seaweed farming
Cultivating seaweed is a major industry in parts of Asia. In Japan, people eat more seaweed than anywhere else in the world. It is cultivated in shallow, coastal seas.

In the Philippines, seaweeds are used to make carrageenan. This is a thickening and binding agent used in sausages, yogurt, shampoos, cosmetics, and toothpastes.

Drugs that could help fight **cancer** *have been extracted from* **sponges**

Salt from the sea
A worker in Thailand rakes sea salt into piles. Extracting the salt is a slow business. Seawater is channeled through a series of shallow ponds where sunshine and wind evaporate the water. This makes the brine (salty water) more and more concentrated. After 18 months, the bed of the final pond is covered in a layer of glistening white salt crystals.

Fish and seafood *farms around the world* provide *us with more than* 53 million *tons of seafood per year*

For safety, waste gas is burned off at the end of a long boom.

Freshwater
Around the world, about 13,000 desalination (desalting) plants produce freshwater from saltwater. They are expensive, but in desert areas they're often the only solution to water shortages. Tw- thirds of the world's desalination plants are in the Middle East—this one is in Dubai.

HOW SALTY IS THE SEA?

You will need: wax paper, baking tray, plastic bottle, seawater, magnifying glass.

Sea water collected during a trip to the coast.

EXPERIMENT

1 LINE THE BAKING TRAY with wax paper. Press the paper down into the corners and turn it up at the edges so that it can hold water.

2 POUR IN ABOUT 1 pint (.5 l) of seawater. Leave the tray in a warm place, such as a pantry or on a sunny window ledge.

3 WHEN ALL THE WATER has evaporated, examine the dried salt crystals under a magnifying glass. Most of the crystals will be cube-shaped.

This shows that: the sea is full of salt minerals. Most of this is the same chemical as table salt.

TOURIST TRAFFIC

A lmost a billion

people now take their vacations overseas every year. Many countries—especially those with beautiful beaches and coral reefs—depend on tourists to provide a living income for their people. But tourism brings problems, too. Building airports, roads, and hotels, providing enough freshwater, and disposing of sewage, all have an effect on coastal environments. Also, the sheer numbers of visitors can threaten local habitats and wildlife. Tourism is important, and here to stay, but it needs to be very carefully planned. Responsible "ecotourism" may help to reduce visitors' impact on the environment.

The human tide

Bournemouth beach, in southern England, is packed with tourists in the summer—up to 100,000 of them on 7 miles (11 km) of sandy beach. Every morning and evening a team of 25 workers with hand rakes and tractor-powered machines cleans the entire beach, shifting up to 22 tons (20 metric tons) of flotsam and litter a day. This clean-up costs huge amounts of money.

Scarce water

Goa, on the west coast of India, is a tourist paradise with long sandy beaches fringed with palm trees. But here, and in many other tropical resorts, there's a price to pay. Big hotels with lush gardens are often allowed to take a huge share of scarce freshwater resources, leaving little for the local people.

A big **hotel** uses as much **electricity** as 3,500 medium-sized **households**

Dangerous sports

Water skiing, power-boating, and jet-skiing are lots of fun, but they can also endanger wildlife. In some vacation resorts they are restricted to certain zones to keep them away from colonies of seals, otters, dolphins, and diving birds, such as cormorants and pelicans.

> " Mediterranean people are becoming increasingly aware that it is not possible to keep using up resources, building up coastal areas, and developing tourism. "

Mediterranean Sustainable
Development Strategy
UNEP, 2005

All visitors to **Belize** are charged a small **fee**— the **money** is used to pay for **nature**

Sea urchin

Starfish

Sea sponge

Beware what you buy

Beautiful shells are for sale on this beach in South Africa. If the trader only collects empty shells for sale, no harm is done, but in many parts of the world, unscrupulous dealers hunt living shellfish, sea turtles, and rare species of starfish, sea urchins, and sponges. If in doubt, do not buy. You could be breaking international laws.

Endangered species

This green sea turtle has hatched on a tropical beach and must dash to the sea past marauding seabirds. Even then it is not safe. Hunters kill adult turtles for meat and shells. Also, when adult females come ashore to lay their eggs, there are more dangers from illegal egg collectors and thoughtless tourists who trespass on protected beaches.

ACTION!

Never be tempted to pick plants or flowers that are growing wild.

Stay on marked paths and keep your distance from wildlife.

Always take litter home with you after a day at the beach.

FOUL SEA

People have been throwing domestic and farm waste into the sea for thousands of years. Long ago, when the world's population was only a few million, this wasn't a problem—there was only a bit of garbage, and the tides and currents soon washed it away. Things are very different now that the world's population is nearly 7 billion. The amount of garbage we're dumping is enormous, and a lot of it is dangerous—industrial chemicals, raw sewage, even nuclear waste. International laws limit many types of dumping at sea, but there's still much to be done in the campaign for cleaner seas.

A supply of **clean water** is essential for all **life**

A thing of the past
The sea turns orange as a ship dumps hundreds of tons of jarosite (the waste product of zinc smelting) off the coast of Australia in 1990. The last permit for this kind of dumping ran out in 1997. No new permits have been issued for dumping industrial waste in Australia's waters.

Mineral waste dumped at sea can sink and kill life on the sea floor.

San Francisco bay contains more than **150 foreign** species carried there in ships' **ballast tanks**

Comb jelly

Alien invaders
When ships unload their cargo, they fill their ballast tanks with seawater to add weight and keep them stable. On arrival at the next port, they pump out the ballast water—teeming with "foreign" marine life. The comb jelly shown here was transported from the North Atlantic to the Black Sea where it has thrived and upset the local ecosystem.

Nuclear dumping

Drum full of low-level nuclear waste

This image shows low-level nuclear waste being dumped in the North Sea. This type of waste includes clothing and equipment contaminated with radioactive chemicals that have been used in hospitals and research laboratories. Although dumping of high-level nuclear waste is already banned, it still happens.

Piped pollution

All over the world, raw sewage is poured into the sea. The sewage feeds bacteria, which multiply and deprive other sea creatures of oxygen. It also contains germs that can cause diseases. The problem is worst in developing countries, where there may be no proper sewage treatment plants.

Bacteria in sewage can cause **fatal diseases** such as **cholera**

" I live in a village called St. Agnes on the coast of north Cornwall, England. My life revolves around surfing and the ocean. I go surfing just about every day and it is really important to me that the sea is kept clean. If it is dirty I am at risk of getting sick from the pollution and sewage, along with all the other animals that swim in the water. I try to help by supporting an environmental group called Surfers Against Sewage, which campaign to clean the seas. SAS has done a lot for the health of the sea and for surfers since it was first set up. "

Brennan Cascelles

Surfers against sewage

The water off our coasts is sometimes so full of bacteria from raw sewage that beaches are closed to the public. Many people campaign to clean up the seas, but the loudest protests have come from surfers—the people who suffer most from illnesses caused by sewage. Their actions have persuaded many goverments to clean up their acts.

Plastic dumped in the oceans **kills** one million **seabirds** and 100,000 **marine mammals** and **turtles** every year

ACTION!

Find out more about organizations that are campaigning for cleaner seas.

Always find out if water is clean before you go swimming in it.

A major sea level rise could affect 72 million people in China alone

RISING SEA LEVELS

Global warming

Scientists tell us that if greenhouse gases such as carbon dioxide carry on increasing in the air as they have been, global average temperature will probably increase by 39°F (4°C) by the end of this century. The last time it was this warm, 125,000 years ago, the polar ice sheets were much smaller, and sea levels were 13–20 ft (4–6 m) higher.

One of the biggest questions that needs to be answered by environmental scientists is "How much will sea levels rise as a result of global warming?" They know that rises in global temperatures will do two things. It will make the water in the oceans expand, so that sea levels will rise a bit. It could also melt some or all of the polar ice caps. This would add huge amounts of water to the oceans, making them rise very much more. The Earth has been warming slowly for 7,000 years. The problem is that human activities over the past 150 years have been making its temperature rise faster and faster.

MELTING ICE CAPS

You will need: 2 identical glass bowls, tray, 2 unopened tin cans, pitcher, water, ice cubes, marker tape.

1 PLACE THE BOWLS on a tray with a can inside each one. Partly fill the first bowl with water, add plenty of ice, and mark the water level with tape. Mark the same level on the second bowl and fill up to the mark with water.

2 PILE ICE CUBES on top of the can in the second bowl, but do not put any ice in the water. You have created one "island" surrounded by "sea ice" and one covered by an "ice cap."

3 LEAVE THE ICE to melt. Notice that the water level in the first bowl is the same, but the "sea level" in the second bowl has risen.

This shows that: when sea ice melts, the water does not take up any extra volume. But when land ice melts, water levels rise.

Cracks in the ice

Over the past few years, huge chunks have broken away from the floating ice shelves around Antarctica. The cause is a rise in sea temperature—and it is a serious warning to us all. When floating ice melts, sea levels do not change. But if the ice caps that cover land start to melt, the world is in trouble because sea levels will rise.

Parts of London could flood if sea levels rise 10 ft (3 m)

The flood threat

If sea level rises by 18 in (.5 m), as predicted by the Intergovernmental Panel on Climate Change, millions of people living near coasts will have to move. Low-lying areas like the Nile Delta, Bangladesh (left), and small islands such as the Maldives will lose much of their best farmland.

GEORGIA
ATLANTIC OCEAN
FLORIDA
Cape Canaveral
GULF OF MEXICO
The Everglades
West Palm Beach
Miami
Florida coastline
Florida after flooding
Florida Keys

Florida's rising sea levels

Low-lying coastal areas around the world are at risk from sea level rise. In Florida (left) a rise of 25 ft (7.5 m) would swamp vast areas of the state, including Miami and West Palm Beach. Elsewhere in the world, cities such as Amsterdam, Bombay, and Sydney would vanish beneath the water.

Half the world's population lives in low-lying coastal areas

Sea defenses

Low-lying, developed countries, such as the Netherlands, already spend huge amounts of money building sea defenses. These walls prevent sea water from spilling onto the land. If sea levels rise they will need to be far higher and cover longer stretches of coast.

Sea wall under construction

Animal WATCH

We share the Earth with millions of other animal species. They all need a place to live that suits them, as well as the right amount of food and water. By destroying or changing habitats, and altering the natural cycles of elements, humans are now causing the extinction of thousands of animal species every year. If things go on as they are, almost a quarter of all the world's mammal species, and one in eight bird species, are likely to be threatened with extinction in the next 25 years.

HABITATS *at risk*

Most living things rely on a particular type of habitat. For example, giant clams are found only in coral reefs, while the world's largest trees—giant sequoias—grow on mountain slopes. Habitats are much more than places to live because they provide everything that different plants or animals need to survive. However, all over the world, habitats are under threat. Some are being destroyed by farming, by logging, or by building, while others are being altered by drainage, pollution, or climate change. Worldwide, loss of habitat is the biggest single threat to wildlife.

" I live in England. I sponsor an elephant named Malaika through a charity called Care For The Wild. Malaika is eight years old and lives in Kenya. She was rescued because she was on land that the villagers lived on. The elephants were there first but the villagers had used the land to grow crops and build homes. When the elephants were on the land, the villagers would kill them. Malaika's parents were killed when she was a baby. Malaika was taken to the Care For The Wild orphanage. "

JQuigley

Tourism

Wherever people travel, habitats may become damaged. These tourists are in Antarctica—one of the remotest destinations on Earth. Antarctica is the cleanest continent, but with more visitors every year, this could change.

Arctic and Antarctica

The polar regions are the last true wildernesses left on Earth, but even here habitat change has taken place. Pipelines now carry oil and gas across the Arctic tundra. Increasing numbers of passenger ships visit Antarctica's shores. More importantly, global warming is melting the polar ice, disrupting the lives of many animals, including penguins.

Adélie penguins need unpolluted seas to survive.

Conservation

Resting in the heat, these rare Asiatic lions live in a protected habitat— the forest in India's Gir National Park. The lions depend on the forest, but it is under threat from farmers who are desperate for land. Shortage of land makes conservation difficult in many parts of the world. Growing enough food for people means less room for wildlife.

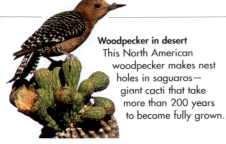

Woodpecker in desert
This North American woodpecker makes nest holes in saguaros—giant cacti that take more than 200 years to become fully grown.

Desert life

Plants in the Sonoran desert (right) can cope with droughts, but they grow much more slowly than plants in most other habitats. If they are damaged—by cars or motorcycles being driven off-road—it can take years for them to recover. Desert animals need plants to survive, so any damage harms them as well.

Tortoise in desert
The rare desert tortoise lives in the US southwest and northern Mexico. It eats desert plants and its shell protects it from the extreme heat.

Coral reef

In this reef off the Bahamas, a plastic bag has caught on some elkhorn coral. Pollution is one of the reasons why the world's coral reefs are in trouble. Reefs are also damaged by dredging and by fishing. Rising sea temperatures—a result of global warming—affect the reefs' algae and disturb the balanced ecosystem.

ACTION!

Do not buy coral or shells—they may have been collected live from a reef.

Do not walk across restricted land in conservation areas.

Wetlands

This marina in Florida was once a coastal wetland—a natural habitat for alligators and wading birds. After forests, wetlands are among the most threatened habitats in the world. Some have been completely destroyed, but others are now protected by an international agreement aimed at conserving wetland life.

Grasslands

At one time, natural grassland covered the whole of the American Midwest and large parts of other continents. However, in the last 100 years, most of the grassland has been plowed up. For grassland animals, such as the prairie dog, there is less space for survival.

The prairie dog's home is in a burrow underground.

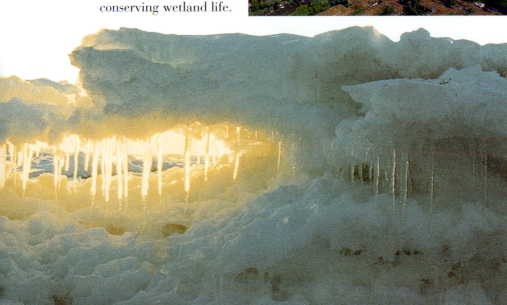

Giant African land snail
This huge snail, reared on Pacific islands as a source of food, escaped into the wild and soon became a serious crop pest.

Alien arrival

The giant African land snail and the *Euglandina* snail were introduced to the Pacific islands of Tahiti and Moorea, in both cases with disastrous results. Alien animals can be introduced in different ways. *Euglandina* was released on purpose. But some animals, like the land snail, escape from captivity. Others arrive by accident, often hidden in ships' cargoes.

Snail-eating snail
To reduce the number of giant African land snails, the *Euglandina rosea* was released on the Pacific islands.

Native snail
Sadly, several species of Pacific *Partula* snails were driven to extinction by the newcomer, *Euglandina rosea.*

Even introduced **pets,** like **cats** and **dogs,** can put native wildlife at **risk**

New species, NEW THREATS

The release of an animal into a habitat where it does not belong can be destructive for the creatures that already live there. Although wild animals are suited to share their homes with certain other animals, the introduction of a newcomer, or "alien" species, can upset nature's balance. An invader is often too powerful a predator or too greedy a consumer of vegetation. The threat from introduced animals is especially serious on islands where wildlife has evolved in isolation. Many of these vulnerable island species are now carefully protected.

Fearsome foxes
In Australia, introduced foxes prey on rare mammals such as the numbat, the bilby, and the stick-nest rat.

No escape

Predatory mammals such as foxes, stoats, rats, and domestic cats are some of the most destructive animals that have been introduced into new habitats. Island creatures often evolve with few natural predators and are not able to hide, run, or fly away.

Hungry stoats
The arrival of stoats in New Zealand almost spelled doom for the takahe, a large but flightless native bird.

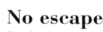

Stowaway rats
Black rats have spread around the world by climbing ships' moorings and hiding on board.

Shelter is becoming hard to find for the rhinoceros iguana.

Nowhere to hide
Native species, such as the rhinoceros iguana of Hispaniola, can be affected when large farm animals are allowed to roam free. In many areas on the island, the scrubby thickets, where the iguana likes to hide, are now eaten and trampled by introduced donkeys and goats.

New competitors
The greater bilby has been driven from parts of Australia by the spread of introduced rabbits, which take over its burrows. Like rabbits, some alien animals harm native wildlife, not by preying on them, but by competing with them for food and shelter.

Alien animals often feed on the eggs and young of native species

The kakapo feeds at night, when predators are less likely to spot it.

Intensive rescue
New Zealand's large, flightless parrot, the kakapo, has been rescued from the brink of extinction. The few remaining birds have been moved from the mainland to nearby islands, where they are safer from predators and can be monitored by conservationists. There are now fewer than a hundred kakapo left in the entire world.

"I live on Maud Island, a refuge for kakapo in New Zealand. There are 18 kakapo on the island, which is free of predators such as cats, stoats, and dogs. When I first met Hoki, the hand-reared kakapo, I sat down quietly and she nibbled on my fingers and chucked sticks at me. At night she would climb onto our roof and it sounded like she was jumping up and down. Hoki was moved to Codfish Island to live in the wild. I haven't seen her since. She has not laid her first eggs yet, but I hope she will have some chicks of her own."

Samantha Paton

Genetic mixing
A different sort of threat faces the rare Simien wolf of Ethiopia. Domestic dogs that have become wild have entered some of the wolf's last remaining refuges, and the two closely related animals have started to breed with each other. Over time, this mixing of genes could mean that the true Simien wolf disappears.

Overhunted animal populations can usually **recover** if their natural **habitats** are not **damaged**

Animal HARVEST

Throughout history, people have hunted animals for food. At first, the harvest of wildlife had little effect on animal populations because, like other predators, humans were few in number. But as towns and cities expanded and commercial hunting became common, the pressure on wild animals increased. Most meat today comes from domesticated, farmed animals, but hunting for food is still important for people in some countries. Where species are threatened, conservationists are trying to persuade people to change their sources of food and to limit hunting so that animals are not killed faster than they breed.

Feeding families

Wild antelopes called duikers are a common source of meat for people in Central Africa. Hunting for "bushmeat" like this poses a threat to wildlife, from crocodiles to chimpanzees. Hunters take wild animals to feed their families or to sell. In places, areas of forest have been picked clean of edible creatures.

Easy target

The Victoria crowned pigeon of New Guinea is under threat because it is hunted for its flesh. At up to 32 in (80 cm) long, this plump bird is the world's largest pigeon. Because it spends most of its time foraging on the forest floor, it is an easy target for hunters.

The sea turns red after a round-up of pilot whales.

Ritual slaughter

Every year, people drive schools of pilot whales into shallow bays around the Faroe Islands, north of Scotland, for mass slaughter. In the past, these annual events provided a much-needed food source for the islanders. Today, there are plenty of alternatives, but many islanders are eager to continue the traditional hunt.

Wildlife farming

Ostriches are commonly bred for their meat in southern Africa, and ostrich farms are now springing up in other parts of the world. This type of animal harvest does not harm wild populations, and is better than taking animals from their natural habitats.

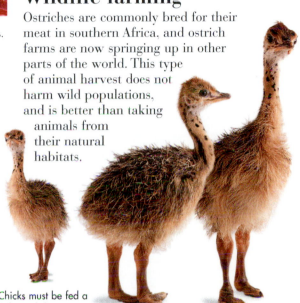

Poached eggs

In Southeast Asia, river turtles called batagurs are caught for their flesh when they come out of the water to lay their eggs. Hunters also dig up the eggs to eat, destroying a whole new generation of these endangered reptiles. Many beaches and riverbanks are now protected during the breeding season.

Chicks must be fed a balanced diet to ensure that they grow properly.

Iguanas, hunted for food in Central America, are now bred in captivity to sustain wild populations

Saved in time

Native Americans hunted bison in North America for thousands of years. Then, in the 19th century, European settlers almost wiped out the animal—a population of 60 million was reduced to 1,000. A few herds were saved, and numbers steadily increased. Today, there are more than 20,000.

> " The tiger survives today thanks to China banning trade in tiger products. "
>
> WORLDWIDE FUND FOR NATURE, 2007

Parts for SALE

Almost every part of the tiger has been revered as a medicine or luxury, including its eyes, whiskers, skin, and bones.

Many animals are not hunted for food, but for their skin, fur, horns, shells, or other

body parts. These animal parts are traded far and wide as decorative objects, ingredients for traditional medicines, or materials for the fashion industry. The wild victims of such trade include many highly endangered species such as big cats, rhinoceroses, gorillas, crocodiles, and sea turtles. Some governments around the world have now made laws to try to control the trade in animal products—but these laws are not easy to enforce.

Traditional medicine

Animals, including Asiatic black bears and tigers, are in danger due to the demands of traditional medicines. Hunters kill bears to collect their gall bladders and other body parts for use in traditional potions. People are now more aware of the illegal trade in animal parts, thanks to the work of organizations such as TRAFFIC. This group aims to ensure that wildlife species are not traded to extinction.

Costly cure

Around 20 million dried seahorses a year are traded for use in traditional chinese medicine. They are caught from the wild by fishermen, who report that seahorse numbers have declined dramatically in recent years. In the shallow seas around South America, the number of seahorses seems to have dropped by 90 percent.

Red fox
With its leg held in a trap, this fox could suffer hours of pain, thirst, hunger, and exposure.

"My name is Artisha, and I live in Chicago, where I am proud to be a young member of PETA (People for the Ethical Treatment of Animals). I am a vegetarian and protest against animals in circuses and the killing of animals for their fur and other body parts. I became a member of PETA because I do not agree with the thoughtless cruelty going on today. The lives of animals are in our hands, and we must take responsibility. Everybody should try to be a peacemaker

Fashion victim

Until recently, chinchillas were caught for their soft fur, used to decorate clothes. The demand for fur still has a terrible effect on many scarce wild mammals. Some are raised in captivity for their fur, but anti-fur campaigners argue that these animals still suffer cruel treatment.

Animal products

It is hard to believe that anybody would want to buy a crocodile skull (top left). But, as with all the objects in this display, it was confiscated by customs officers from vacationers on their way home. These souvenirs were the result of hunting threatened animals. If people stop buying illegal animal products, poachers will stop providing them.

The **Siamese crocodile** is **extinct** in parts of **Southeast Asia** as a result of **trade** in its **hide**

Customs seizures

Officials seized these jaguar skins as they were being smuggled out of Brazil. The CITES (Convention on the International Trade in Endangered Species) treaty is a set of rules that limits the trade in animals and animal products. These rules aim to stop endangered species from being taken from one country to another and help to protect wild species. But some people still risk breaking the law if the price is right.

Many countries now have laws controlling trade in rare and exotic animals

PET *trade*

Popularity can be dangerous for wild animals. Lots of people like to keep exotic, or foreign, creatures as pets or for collections, but the trade has helped bring about the decline of some wildlife species. High-value rare animals are snatched from the wild, smuggled long distances in cramped containers, and sold illegally through pet stores and dealers. Strict laws and undercover investigations are two ways to regulate the trade. Another is for people who buy the animals to make sure that they come from approved sources.

Operation Chameleon, an investigation in the US, has stopped many **reptile smugglers** from trading

Red-kneed tarantula
These Mexican spiders make interesting pets, but wild populations are declining due to the pet trade.

Cage birds
Gouldian finches have declined in the wild in Australia partly because large numbers of them have been trapped for sale as pets.

Animal trappers

Red-kneed tarantulas and gouldian finches are two species of animal harmed by the pet trade. The rarer a species gets, the more demand there is for it. Trappers steal young birds from their nests and dig spiders, like tarantulas, out of their burrows.

Squashed snakes
Burmese pythons are sometimes transported hidden in suitcases. Hundreds of young snakes may be squashed into one bag.

Smuggled victims
These macaws were smuggled from South America in cramped conditions. In 2007, the European Union banned the import of wild birds, for fear that diseases like bird flu could be carried this way. Before that, 90 percent of traded wild birds were sold in Europe, so the ban saves the lives of many wild and rare birds.

Difficult pets
Reptiles, such as this Burmese python, are shipped across the world to live in conditions totally different from their tropical homes. To stay healthy, reptiles need special light to simulate sunlight, warm temperature conditions, and the right food. Many owners find exotic pets too demanding and neglect or abandon them.

At least 58 species of parrot are at risk as a direct result of the pet trade

Swallowtail birdwing butterfly

Queen Alexandra birdwing butterfly

Reared for market
Villagers in Papua New Guinea have set up caterpillar gardens and hatching cages to raise large numbers of spectacular birdwing butterflies for export to collectors. Breeding in captivity satisfies the demand for exotic animals without plundering wild populations.

ACTION!
Keep pets that you can care for properly—tropical animals need special conditions and may live for a long time.

Write to a group that campaigns against illegal trade in exotic pets, and see if you can help.

Saved in time
The Sepilok Rehabilitation Center in Borneo cares for orangutans that have been confiscated from smugglers. They are looked after until they are ready for release back into their forest home. Efforts to return these orangutans to the wild are not easy. The rescued animals are often in poor health, stressed, and far from their original habitat.

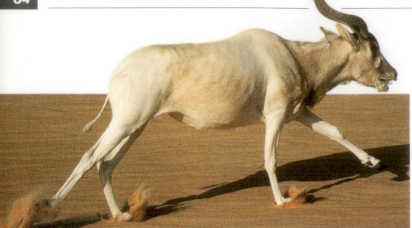

Hunted down

After years of being hunted for sport and for their prized horns, fewer than 200 addax still roam the deserts of North Africa. Although they are swift runners, they cannot easily escape when chased across the sands by hunters in vehicles. These, and many other hoofed animals of the open country, are still at risk from hunting.

Safari hunters will pay $9,000 for a license to shoot one elephant

Hunting controls can make the difference between survival and extinction for threatened animals

Hunting
for sport

Safari income

The hunter who shot this Cape buffalo in Zimbabwe did so legally. Some southern African countries allow hunting in reserves because it can benefit conservation. Tourists pay to collect their animal trophies. Some of the money is then put back into the reserve as funds for the upkeep of the land and its animal inhabitants.

Wild animals have been hunted for the thrill of the sport since ancient times. Today, all sorts of people go shooting or fishing for fun. Hunting as a hobby does not always damage wildlife populations, but many people think it is wrong to kill an animal for amusement. Careless or excessive hunting can be cruel to animals, and can push rare species closer to extinction. Some conservationists argue that controlled hunting in reserves and private parks can help to protect natural habitats, and even the species that are hunted there—the species are better protected because the hunting brings in money.

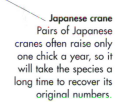

Toxic shot

When hunters shoot birds, they often use lead shot. After they've gone, many small lead pellets are left on the ground. These are poisonous to other birds like ducks, which often eat them by mistake, thinking they're pieces of grit. In some areas, shooting with lead is now banned.

" I live in Treviso in Italy. From my bedroom window I can see and hear many birds—small ones like robins, woodpeckers, and pigeons, but also big ones like woodcocks and pheasants. A few miles from my house is a place where storks nest during their migration. In the breeding season I hear hunters shooting and see them with their rifles and dogs. I hope all the birds shelter in my yard and that the hunters find nothing. I like birds because they are free to fly in the sky. Maybe one day the hunting will be banned and there will be even more birds around my house. "

Alessandro Carboni

About **100,000 birds of prey** are **shot** in **Malta** every year

Japanese crane
Pairs of Japanese cranes often raise only one chick a year, so it will take the species a long time to recover its original numbers.

Success story

In the 1920s, European visitors to Japan hunted the Japanese crane close to extinction. Only 20 of the birds were left. The crane was then given protection from the sport hunters, and its numbers have now risen to about 600. Changes in people's attitudes play an important part in the race to save rare animals from extinction through overhunting.

Fishing for fun

Sport fishing is big business in places like Hawaii. Although angling is one of the most accepted forms of hunting, it can reduce fish populations if people do not follow the rules. In the US, laws protect rare species of fish, such as the striped bass, Nassau grouper, and sturgeon.

Leatherback turtle
Warm tropical oceans. Estimated numbers left: 25,000—30,000 females. Trapped in fishing nets, hunted for their flesh and eggs, and killed by plastic bags.

Common sturgeon
Precise numbers not known, but may now be extinct from 28 European countries where it used to be found, including Spain, Russia, and Iceland.

Black rhinoceros
Central and southern Africa. Estimated numbers left: 2,500. Hunted for their horns (used in medicine), and habitat destroyed for agriculture.

St. Helena earwig
St. Helena, South Atlantic. This creature was last seen in 1967, and experts now fear it to be extinct.

Animals IN DANGER

*Up to **a dozen** species of insect become **extinct** every day*

A ll over the world, wild animals are faced with an increasing struggle to survive. Deciding which species are most threatened, and how we can help them, is one of the most important tasks facing biologists today. Many endangered species are protected by laws against hunting and by international agreements that stop them from being sold. In extreme cases, some have even been brought back from the brink of extinction by breeding them in captivity and releasing their young back into the wild. But for most wild animals, the best safeguard is an unspoiled natural habitat. If they have this, they can look after themselves.

Clones without homes

The giant panda is probably the world's most famous endangered animal. It lives in the bamboo forests of China, a habitat that is steadily shrinking as the land is taken over for farming and building houses. Some scientists think that pandas can be saved by cloning, which would increase their numbers by producing young animals from a mother's cells. But without the bamboo forest, cloned pandas could not survive in the wild.

Bali starling
Bali, Indonesia
Estimated numbers left: 1,000 in zoos, fewer than 10 in the wild.

In the red
Endangered species are monitored by the International Union for the Conservation of Nature (IUCN). This organization publishes "Red Lists" of endangered animals and plants, showing how much danger they are in. These five animals (left) are on the "critically endangered" list—the highest category of threat. Without help, they could soon become extinct.

Big and beautiful
Big cats are beautiful and glamorous. This means that when they are threatened, they make the headlines and attract funds for their protection. Although it is endangered, the leopard is not at the point of extinction. But its close relative the tiger may soon become extinct in the wild.

If these sand eels are threatened, the puffin is also vulnerable.

Not so cute
This puffin has a beakful of sand eels—small fish that it depends on for its food. Sand eels are not beautiful or glamorous, but without them puffins would find it difficult to survive. Today, sand eels are threatened by new and more efficient fishing techniques. To look after puffins, we have to look after their food sources, too.

Keeping count
Using an inflatable raft slung beneath a balloon, scientists survey treetop wildlife in a West African forest. Their work will show what lives in the trees, and how the numbers might be affected by changes to the environment. Many specimens collected in surveys like this are species that have never been seen before.

Safety offshore
The tuatara is a unique lizard-like reptile that comes from New Zealand. It has been harmed by introduced species—particularly rats, which eat its eggs and its young. Today, tuataras survive only on about 30 small, offshore islands, where rats are kept under control.

Scientists believe that **50,000** species a year are becoming **extinct,** so we are in the middle of a **mass extinction** like the one that killed the **dinosaurs.**

ACTION!
Join a conservation group that campaigns to protect wild animals.

If you are buying a pet, make sure it is one that has been bred in captivity, not caught in the wild.

Do not pay to watch performing animals that have been taken from the wild.

Parks and RESERVES

All shapes and sizes

Yosemite National Park in California covers 1,865 sq miles (3,000 sq km) and is home to rare animals, such as the puma, the black bear, and the great gray owl. However, smaller pond, woodland, and meadow reserves are just as important.

National parks, nature reserves, and other protected places are areas of land, or sometimes sea, that are set aside for nature conservation. They are important refuges for wildlife. Park staff work hard to protect the environment and the animals that live there. Because parks and reserves preserve whole habitats, they benefit a range of different species. But these areas are not always popular with local people because they may stop them from using the land for their own needs.

ACTION!

Visit a nature reserve and see if you can join volunteers who are helping with conservation work.

Find out more about organizations that support wild animal reserves.

Elephant trouble

National parks have played an important role in conserving African elephants. In some parks, elephant herds have become so large that they have begun to damage the parks' vegetation. Occasionally, staff have to shoot, or cull, some animals to reduce numbers and prevent overcrowding.

Success story

Parks set up in the Andes Mountains, South America, have helped to save the vicuña, a relative of the camel. In 1965, only 6,000 vicuñas remained, due to hunting for their fleece. Now safe from poachers, their numbers have risen to almost 100,000.

Parks and people

This tourist guide in a reserve in Madagascar is tempting a ring-tailed lemur into the open for visitors. Protected areas like this can provide jobs in tourism for local people who can no longer hunt or clear land for farming to make a living. Conservationists are trying to find more ways to ease the hardship that parks can cause for local communities.

Animal guards
Some ex-poachers now work as guards so that they can make a living without hunting protected animals.

There are almost **50,000** animal **parks** and reserves in the **world**

" I live in Cape Town in South Africa, and last week I visited Pilanesburg National Park. We saw impala, wildebeest, birds, and springbok. Then, right in front of us was an elephant. He had no idea we were watching him eat and knock down trees! That huge gray animal will stay in my mind forever. Last of all, we saw hippos. Using binoculars we could watch them playing in the water. I had a terrific day at Pilanesburg, and I think we should work together to protect these animals so that people in the future can enjoy seeing them, too. " Maya Schkolne

Extreme measures

Armed guards, like this one from Kenya, patrol some parks to protect animals from people who enter illegally to hunt or poach wildlife. Such drastic measures show how serious the clash between conservation and people can be. In some places, whole villages have been moved to make way for parks, causing resentment among local people.

Park life
Most African elephants now live in national parks like the Serengeti in Tanzania.

The **Pulau Ubin** reserve in Singapore has **saved** the native **fruit bat** from **extinction**

ZOO DEBATE

Panda controversy
People disagree about whether giant pandas should be kept in zoos. They are popular exhibits, but in the past have been taken from the wild to satisfy zoos' demands. The species is now under threat of extinction, and breeding in zoos may save it. However, it is difficult to breed giant pandas in captivity.

Zoos containing wild animals have been around since ancient times, and today there are more than 10,000 zoos throughout the world. For many years, animal lovers and conservationists have campaigned to improve the conditions in which animals are kept. They have helped to bring about important changes at many zoos, but there are still lots of places where animals are kept in terrible conditions. Today, there is heated debate about what the proper role of zoos should be, and some people believe that keeping animals in zoos of any kind is wrong.

ACTION!
Contact a group campaigning to improve conditions for animals in zoos and find out about their work.

Adopt a zoo animal—you will help pay for its care and also learn about the animal.

At least **20 animal** species owe their **survival** to **conservation** in **zoos**

New zoos
Many modern zoos provide natural, spacious enclosures for their animals, with trees to climb and places to hide. Large creatures, such as rhinos, can live in groups and behave much as they would in the wild. Until recently, home to most zoo animals was a bare cage with a concrete floor and metal bars.

Roaming rhinos
Rhinoceroses are able to roam in the spacious, seminatural enclosures at San Diego Wild Animal Park in California.

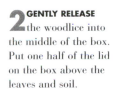

Amusement or education

At one time, zoos used to dress chimpanzees in clothes and make them perform to amuse visitors. Today, more and more zoos are trying to educate people about wildlife instead of just entertaining them. They show visitors how animals behave naturally and provide information about conservation.

> " Our own future lies in the preservation of other creatures. "

ZOOCHECK

Saved by zoos

Przewalski's wild horse is an ancestor of the domestic horse. It would have died out long ago if herds had not been preserved in zoos in Eurasia and North America. The species became extinct in the wild in 1968, but a captive herd had been established several decades earlier. The species has since survived in zoos through 14 generations, and some horses have been released into the wild in parts of Eastern Europe. The total population today is about 2,000.

WOODLICE WORLD

EXPERIMENT

You will need: an old shoe box, scissors, protective gloves, damp leaves and soil, cotton, about 10 woodlice*— you will find them outside under stones, plant pots, and dead leaves.

1 CUT THE LID OF THE shoe box in half. Place a pile of damp leaves and soil at one end of the box and some dry cotton at the other end.

2 GENTLY RELEASE the woodlice into the middle of the box. Put one half of the lid on the box above the leaves and soil.

3 PLACE THE BOX in a bright place and watch the woodlice. They should all go to the dark and damp end of the box, and ignore the dry cotton at the light end of the box.

Within seconds, the woodlice decide which way to go.

This shows that: animals are happiest in conditions that are most like their natural habitat. Woodlice like damp and dark places and are not happy in light and dry conditions.

*Put the woodlice back outside when the experiment is over.

Zoos to the rescue

The California condor almost became extinct in the wild as a result of egg-collecting and pesticide poisoning, but it now flies free again. This is because zoos in California bred birds for release into the wild, where the condor still needs protection. Zoos play an important role in conservation.

Food WATCH

Producing food for everybody on Earth without damaging the environment is a real challenge, especially since people in many places are becoming richer and wanting to eat more meat and more varied diets. Distributing the food fairly is complicated and difficult, too. At the moment, many of those who live in rich countries eat too much, while hundreds of thousands of men, women, and children in poor countries don't get enough to eat.

FOOD FOR ALL

Airborne attack

Skimming over a field in California, a plane sprays pesticides on the crop below. Pesticides help farmers to produce big harvests, but they have harmful side effects. They often kill useful animals as well as pests, and they also end up in our food.

Colorado beetle grubs

Pest alert

Colorado beetle grubs eat potato and tomato leaves. For pests like these, big fields provide an almost endless supply of food.

With more people than ever on Earth, we need all the food we can grow. During the last 50 years, scientists have developed many ways to boost harvests so that we get more from the land that is farmed. Heavy machinery makes light work of jobs that once took weeks, while fertilizers and pesticides help to produce record yields. Special breeding programs have improved the crops, and genetic engineering may improve them even more. However, this kind of farming has drawbacks. Unlike traditional farming, it has a big effect on wildlife and may also reduce the natural fertility of the soil. Used wisely, the land can support both farming and wildlife.

Harvest mouse nibbling on a plant stem

Battery hens

These chickens will spend their lives in small cages that allow thousands of them to be raised side by side. Intensive farming of this kind makes eggs cheap, but the chickens suffer because they have no room to move.

Lost wildlife

Many wild animals, such as this harvest mouse, are harmed by modern farming methods. In Europe, harvest mice were once common in cereal fields. Today, their nests are often destroyed by combine harvesters, making it hard for them to survive.

Natural help

On organic farms, like this one in England, artificial pesticides are never used. Instead, pests are controlled by swapping the crops around each year, and by using some plants to lure pests away from others. Here, rows of potato plants are growing next to mustard, which has bright yellow flowers. The mustard plants act only as a decoy to attract flying insects away from the potatoes.

Organic farming works with nature rather than against it

Asian organics

Organic farming is not a new idea—in some places it has been used for thousands of years. On traditional Chinese farms, manure from farm animals is used to keep the soil fertile. Additionally, waste food is used to raise pigs, poultry, and fish.

A combine harvester works fast and can reap the crop while the grain is at its best.

The wheat is emptied into a tractor-drawn trailer.

Large-scale farming

These wheat fields in the US produce huge harvests that help to feed people around the world. But this kind of intensive farming causes problems for the environment. It relies heavily on pesticides and other agricultural chemicals that damage the soil. It also uses fossil fuels to drive farm machinery.

Traces of pesticide can be found in almost all of the non-organic food that we eat

Each year the world's farmers use more than 165 million tons of artificial fertilizer

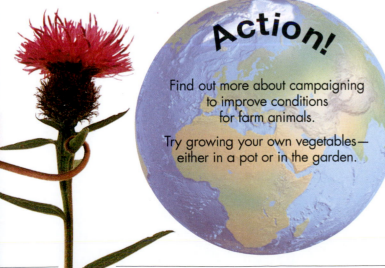

Action!

Find out more about campaigning to improve conditions for farm animals.

Try growing your own vegetables—either in a pot or in the garden.

Genetically modified crops

Although they look like ordinary plants, these soybeans have been given extra genes that make them easier to grow. Many scientists believe that such genetically modified (GM) crops will help farmers grow more food without harming the environment. Others are concerned that they may cause problems by passing on the new genes to plants in the wild.

Uneven

Poor harvest

Farmers in many developing countries suffer poor harvests from their dry, infertile soils. Fertilizers can help, but they are expensive, and many farmers rely on supplies donated by aid agencies. Lack of money also means that almost all of the farm labor must be done by hand.

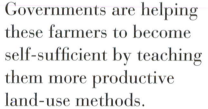

Farmers have the means of producing more food while still protecting the environment

Rich harvest

A bumper crop of sweet peppers pours into a trailer behind a harvester on a farm in California. This is "intensive" farming—producing very high yields by using modern methods. Soil fertility has been boosted by fertilizers, and chemical sprays have kept pests and crop diseases away. The high value of the crop provides the profits the farmer needs to invest in expensive harvesting machines and agricultural chemicals.

Farmers in the rich and fertile regions of the world are

fortunate because they can produce an abundance of food. Even if their crops are not needed immediately, the harvests can be preserved and sold later. However, excess fresh food often goes to waste because it is unwanted where it is grown. In contrast, farmers in the world's poorest countries struggle with infertile soils and a lack of water for little return. When their crops fail they have no money to buy imported food. Governments are helping these farmers to become self-sufficient by teaching them more productive land-use methods.

Harvest

Storage problems

In parts of Africa, up to a quarter of all stored grain is damaged by mold, weevils, or rodents. This raised corn silo in KwaZulu-Natal, South Africa, is the only way farmers can store their precious corn harvest. Many international aid programs are helping villagers to design and build better storage containers.

Halving the amount lost in storage could save more than 30 million tons of grain a year

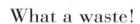

Rodent pests
Rats and mice eat tons of stored grain every year.

What a waste!

Until recently, governments in rich countries paid farmers to produce as much food as they could, whether it was wanted or not. This led to huge surpluses, and a great deal of food was wasted. In California, these oranges were left to rot, while in Europe, milk was left to go sour, and thousands of tons of butter were stockpiled.

Preserving the food

Developed countries have many ways of preserving food so that it remains in perfect condition for months or even years. Food processing and packaging enables supermarkets to stock their shelves all year round. It also allows producers to export foods to other countries.

Bottling
Pickled tomatoes, gherkins, even eggs, can be stored in air-tight jars like this.

Freezing
Fruit and vegetables, like these peas, can be washed, frozen, and packed within hours of being picked on the farm.

Canning
Fruit, fish, beans, and many other foods will last for years in sealed metal cans.

Smoking
For thousands of years, people have preserved fish and meat by smoking.

Drying
Sun- or machine-dried fruits keep their flavor and nutritional value.

The Feed MACHINE

In Canada, summer **wheat** harvests are 25 percent **bigger** in areas where there are natural **windbreaks**

Only farming on a huge scale can produce the vast amounts of grain and crops needed for human food and animal feed. But this kind of farming can have a large impact on the environment. When trees and bushes are removed to make way for giant farm machines, the soil and crops are left with no protection from the wind, and local wildlife can lose their homes. The chemicals used to fertilize the soil and control pests and diseases may also cause harm by poisoning innocent species and by leaking into nearby rivers.

Grain production

In Oregon, the wheat crop is gathered in by combine harvesters. These giant machines provide the most efficient way of harvesting grain crops from huge fields. However, their large engines are powered by diesel fuel. They have huge tanks, often holding more than 265 gallons (1,000 liters) of fuel, and burning this adds to the greenhouse effect.

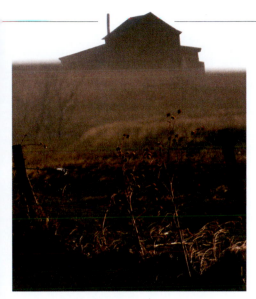

Wind damage

In some parts of the world, a serious environmental problem with very large fields is that once the crop is harvested, the soil is left bare and vulnerable. In long spells of hot weather, the precious topsoil soon dries out. A strong wind can blow away hundreds of tons of soil in a matter of hours.

Hedge hideaway

Hedgerows on farmland help to preserve the environment. The dense foliage shields crops and soil from wind damage and the tangled roots help to anchor the soil and conserve water. Hedges are the last stronghold of many rare wild flowers. They also provide living spaces for various species of insects, birds, reptiles, and mammals.

Red Admiral butterflies lay eggs on nettles, the main food of their caterpillars.

Blue tits nest in hedges and feed their young on grubs and caterpillars.

Rabbits burrow into banks and under hedges.

A typical hedge can support 20 bird species and 50-60 different plants

Chemical spraying

Many people worry about the number of chemicals used on farms. Crops may be sprayed with fertilizers to help them grow well, herbicides to kill weeds, fungicides to stop molds, and insecticides to control harmful insects. But people cannot have it both ways. It is chemicals such as these that provide us with large, unblemished fruits and vegetables at reasonable prices.

Action!

Support organizations that encourage more wildlife in the countryside.

Join a group of volunteers to keep local hedges free of litter.

Find out how organic food is grown without the use of chemicals.

Even delicate crops like tomatoes can be harvested by machine.

Smart machines

Specialized machines, like this tomato harvester, have replaced most of the people who once worked on farms in developed countries. They are expensive, but much faster than human workers. But heavy machines can damage the soil by packing it down so that air and water cannot pass through it freely. Most farm machines have huge balloon tires to minimize this problem.

FAMINE!

All around the world, millions die from hunger each year, and from diseases caused by poor diet and lack of clean drinking water. Drought is one cause of famine—when water is scarce, crops perish and leave the population without food. Natural disasters like floods, hurricanes, and diseases also destroy crops and livestock over huge areas. Wars are another cause. Armies drive farmers from their land and burn their fields to starve people into defeat. Whenever famine strikes, international aid agencies respond quickly with emergency food to help people survive until new crops can be grown.

Failed catch
The 2007 drought that hit Sichuan, China, devastated both fishing and farming in the province.

Famine relief

When drought, crop failure, soaring prices, and restricted access to food cause widespread famine in Ethiopia, starving people have to depend on international relief organizations. Here, grain from the World Food Program is being distributed near Guguftu, in the north of the country.

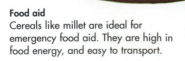

Food aid
Cereals like millet are ideal for emergency food aid. They are high in food energy, and easy to transport.

Flooded land

Disaster struck in 2000 when the Limpopo River burst its banks in Mozambique, destroying crops over a large area and washing away crops and grain supplies. At the same time, an estimated 100,000 people were trapped on rooftops and in trees after severe flooding in the central part of the country.

Drop zone
The 2006 food shortage in Indonesia was caused, not by drought or flood, but by a devastating earthquake. Here, supplies are being dropped by Indonesian military forces.

Airborne aid

An air drop from a cargo plane is often the only way to get emergency food quickly to the victims of famine. Before food supplies can be transported overland, large numbers of trucks and fuel need to be available. Even then, the going can be slow and difficult in disaster areas where roads have become impassable.

> **" In 2007, the World Food Program fed more than 86 million people in 80 countries. "**

UNITED NATIONS
WORLD FOOD PROGRAM

ACTION!

Take part in a sponsored event to raise funds for famine victims.

Watch the news and discuss famine issues at school or with friends.

Give a week's allowance to a good cause.

Refugee crisis

In 1999, thousands of people were forced to flee their homes to escape from the fierce fighting in Kosovo. Many of the war refugees became trapped in the countryside with no means of obtaining food. Aid agencies used helicopters to deliver bread and other foodstuffs to groups of hungry refugees.

Protecting wildlife

Many crop farmers leave a wide band of natural vegetation around the edge of their fields. Along with hedges, trees, and woods, these pesticide-free wildlife reserves are rich in the grasses and flowers that provide food sources and shelter for insects, birds, and animals.

Frogs
Populations of frogs help farmers to control slugs–a major crop pest.

Hedgehogs
In natural areas, hedgehogs flourish and prey on slugs and insects.

Birds
Thrushes and other birds thrive on wild areas of farmland, where they feed on snails and insects.

Working with Nature

Action!

Start a compost heap at home to save on plant fertilizer and improve the soil in your garden.

See what organic foods are available in your local supermarket. Meat and dairy products can be organic, too.

Many farmers in the developed world are turning away from using pesticides and fertilizers and are growing food more naturally. Organic farming produces smaller harvests than intensive farming and, as a result, produce can be more expensive. However, some consumers are happy to pay a bit extra in return for chemical-free foods. Farmers in developing countries with poor soils can also increase their food production by growing combinations of crops. This farming method protects the land by putting nutrients back into the soil, and also conserves the environment.

Animal manure can be sprayed from a tank mounted on a tractor.

Recycling natural fertilizers

Farmers often keep animals and spread their manure on the land. This is a natural source of nitrogen and other chemicals that crops need for healthy growth. Soil fertility can also be improved by digging in composted plant remains and growing a mixture of crops in a rotation system.

Farming with trees

In hot climates, where the Sun can dry out the soil and scorch young crops, many farmers are choosing to grow trees in their fields. This system is called agroforestry. Rows of papaya trees provide excellent shade and wind protection for this field of corn in Polynesia. The farmer can harvest fruit from the trees as well as his cereal crop.

Papaya fruit

NATURAL RECYCLING

You will need: 1 red pepper, knife, polyethelene food bag, bag tie.

1 CUT THE PEPPER in half. Use one half for the experiment and leave it uncovered for a few hours. This will allow microscopic mold spores in the air to land on the soft inner surface of the pepper.

2 PLACE THE PEPPER inside a bag and seal it with a bag tie. Leave the bag in a warm place.

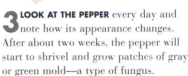

3 LOOK AT THE PEPPER every day and note how its appearance changes. After about two weeks, the pepper will start to shrivel and grow patches of gray or green mold—a type of fungus.

This shows that: when a plant dies, the remains are quickly broken down by fungi, bacteria, and other tiny organisms. In nature, this rotting process returns all the plant's nutrients to the soil.

> ❝ Wildlife is not a luxury for the organic farmer, but an essential part of the farming system. ❞
>
> SOIL ASSOCIATION

Organic food sales are growing faster than any other area of the food market

Rearing ducks in rice paddies helps to control insect pests.

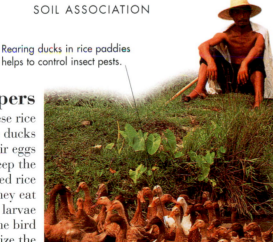

Animal helpers

Many Chinese rice farmers also raise ducks and geese for their eggs and meat. They keep the birds in flooded rice paddies, where they eat weeds and insect larvae (grubs). The bird droppings fertilize the fields. Some Asian farmers stock their rice paddies with fish as an extra source of food.

Double crop benefits

Farmers can improve poor soils by "intercropping." This means growing one crop alongside a different crop. Here, spring wheat produces grain. The alternating rows of beans provide food, plus leaves for animal feed. They also improve the soil by producing nitrogen—a natural fertilizer.

GM benefits

The corn in this field looks the same as any other, but it has been given extra genes (genetically modified) to make it resistant to an all-purpose weedkiller. This means that instead of spraying the crop several times with different herbicides, the farmer can spray the field just once. The weeds are killed, and the crop remains unharmed. By reducing the use of chemicals, GM technology can benefit the environment.

GM Food Debate

> ## "Biotechnology will be a key factor in improving the quality and quantity of the food supply."
>
> JOHN WOOD
> UK FOOD AND DRINK FEDERATION

Scientists can now alter the characteristics of crops by splicing genes from one plant into a totally unrelated plant—something that cannot be done by traditional plant breeding. With this new biotechnology, scientists hope to create genetically modified (GM) crops that will be naturally resistant to insect pests and diseases, grow in very dry soils, contain more food energy or vitamins, or simply taste better and stay fresh longer. But GM technology has created a stormy debate. While some people believe it could help solve world hunger, others are concerned about its possible harmful effects on people and the environment.

Changing nature

This scientist is studying a genetically modified tomato plant in a research laboratory. In one type of GM tomato, scientists have altered the genes that cause overripe fruit to wrinkle and go soft. The modified fruits stay firm, fresh, and appetizing for much longer than ordinary tomatoes.

GM risks

One of the main concerns about GM crops is that pollen from them might cross-pollinate with GM-free crops and wild plants of similar species. Also, in the UK, ecologists have shown that more animal and plants live in ordinary crop fields than in fields of GM crops resistant to all-purpose weed killers. Some people are worried, too, that GM foods could be bad for our health in some way or cause allergies.

GM corn requires far less spraying with chemicals to control weeds in the crop.

Bees and other insects might carry pollen from GM plants to other plants, and alter them, too.

" I'm Mike from Exton, Pennsylvania. I believe that we should research GM food, because it has great potential to help mankind. But it is not yet perfected and should not be marketed until it's 100 percent safe. I'm concerned that new foods could cause allergies and other health risks. Another danger is that GM "super crops" may cross-breed and create "super weeds," which could wipe out other native plants. The release of these GM foods could do more harm than good if they are not completely safe. "

Mike Baney

Food research

Experts hope the addition of long-life genes to these tomatoes will help reduce food waste. In other tests, scientists have added the vitamin A gene to a variety of rice grown in Asia. This should help local people, who suffer blindness through lack of this vitamin in their diet. Other laboratories are working on drought-resistant crops to help farmers in Africa who are plagued by lack of rainfall.

Clear labels

Now grown around the world, GM soybeans and corn are found in many processed foods. In Europe, Japan, and Australia, food with GM ingredients has to be labeled so consumers can choose whether to buy the products or not. Labeling does not, however, extend to meat and dairy products that come from animals fed on GM products.

" **I believe the risks to the environment, human health, and agriculture are irreversible.** "

DR. SUE MEYER
GENEWATCH

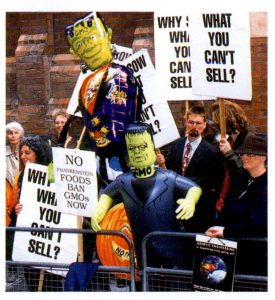

World protest

All around the world, people protested that GM foods were introduced too quickly, without enough safety testing. People were also worried that patents (ownership rights) on GM crops gave biotechnology companies too much power. Many governments have now brought in tight controls, and companies have to work hard to prove their GM crops are beneficial.

Livestock FARMING

ACTION!

Ask your school to arrange a visit to a working livestock farm.

Discuss with your friends the issues of animal welfare on farms.

Find out more about the meat and eggs that you eat.

In some farming systems, large numbers of animals are raised on a very small area of land. The animals may be kept in pens or sheds and fed with specially prepared animal food, instead of being allowed to graze on open fields. This method of meat production is called intensive farming, although people who disapprove of the system call it "factory farming." The animals are well-fed and are checked frequently for any health problems, but some people feel it is wrong—or even cruel—to keep animals in such confined spaces.

Most **beef cattle** reared on **feedlots** in the **US** never see **grass**

Battery or free range?

Many large-scale egg producers keep hens in "battery" units. These are huge sheds containing up to 10,000 birds in small stacked cages. Food and water arrive through automatic dispensers, and the eggs roll onto a conveyor belt to be washed and packed. Producers claim this is the only way of meeting the demand for cheap eggs, but from 2012, it will be against the law in Europe.

Free-range hens
These hens are free to roam and feed on grass shoots and insects as well as chicken-feed.

Battery hens
Hens kept in these cages can barely turn around and live entirely on a scientifically controlled diet.

Cattle in feedlots

To satisfy the demand for cheap beef and burgers, millions of cattle in the US are fattened up in enclosures called feedlots. These cattle may be given hormones in their feed to make them put on weight faster as well as antibiotics to prevent infections. This farming practice is not followed worldwide and is banned in the UK.

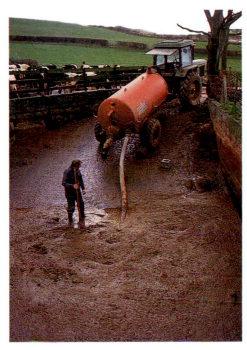

> ❝ I live in the suburbs of Paris in France. The meat we eat in our school lunches comes from factory farms. It upsets me to know that these animals are locked up indoors and live squashed together. I like to eat at my grandma's because she buys her eggs and chickens from free-range farms. These taste delicious! I encourage my family to buy free-range meat because these animals can run around in the fields and have a less stressful life. It's better for them and for us! ❞
>
> *Morgane Billy*

A smelly problem

The slurry, or animal waste, from cattle, pig, and poultry farms is often collected and sprayed onto fields as natural manure. However, there is a limit as to how much can be used. Farmers have to be careful not to spread too much slurry, since potassium, nitrogen, and phosphates in the manure can pollute nearby rivers and lakes.

Some **animal slurry** is turned into clean, **safe** garden **fertilizer**

Fattening up

Intensive pig farmers fatten up young pigs on mixtures containing foods like grain, fish-meal, bone-meal, and skimmed milk. The animals are reared indoors in warm, well-ventilated sheds. Small groups of pigs may be kept in separate pens to prevent fighting.

Huge concrete silos contain stocks of animal feed—a mixture of grain, soybeans, and fish-meal from South America.

Mountains of grain are grown and harvested in the surrounding fields.

Fishing for **Food**

Competing for fish

Mauritanian fishers once had their coastal fishing grounds to themselves and were able to catch a plentiful supply of golden mullet. Today, these fishers have to compete with illegal trawlers from Europe and other faraway places. As well as reducing West Africa's fish stocks, the poachers are taking essential food from local people.

Fish provide people with a healthy source of food protein. In Japan, fish accounts for 60 percent of the protein people eat, and in rural parts of Africa, river and lake fish are often the only source of protein available. Small-scale local fishing does no harm to the environment, but intensive fishing by deep-water trawlers in some areas is threatening to wipe out fish populations. Governments now put strict quotas or limits on the numbers of fish that can be caught in many fishing grounds. This action aims to conserve the world's endangered fish stocks for future generations.

Factory trawlers

The trawl nets used by this North Sea fishing boat can scoop up a ton of fish at a time. The nets used by deep-sea supertrawlers can take 100 tons in a single sweep. This devastating efficiency has caused some fish populations to fall dangerously low.

A winch is used to haul the bulging nets back on board.

Fish or forest?

Shrimp farming has provided a new source of food for people in southeast Asia. The shrimp also fetch a good price when they are sold to wealthy countries. However, the creation of these fish ponds means cutting down coastal mangrove forests, which protect the shore and provide breeding grounds for other fish.

Mangrove trees protect the coast from erosion and storm damage.

Shrimp are cooked and frozen for export.

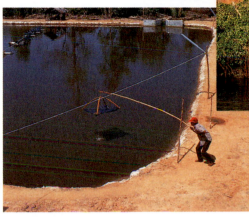

Shrimp farms now replace half of all Thailand's mangrove forests.

> **Scientists predict permanent collapse of all commercial fish species within 50 years, if action is not taken to reverse overfishing.**
>
> OCEANA, 2008

ACTION!

Only buy canned tuna marked "dolphin friendly" on the label—some tuna nets trap dolphins as well.

Discuss with your friends whether it makes sense to use so much fish as animal food.

Find out where the fish you eat comes from.

Fish-meal industry

Do cows eat fish? Surprisingly, the answer is "yes." And so do pigs, hens, and other farm animals. Nearly half of all the fish caught worldwide is processed into fish-meal for use as animal feed. This factory in Peru helps to turn almost the whole of the country's fish catch into meal for the beef cattle of North America.

Traditional hunters

For centuries, sea mammals have provided the Inuit people of North America with the essentials of life—meat, skins for clothing, bones for harpoon heads, and blubber for lamps. Most Inuit now live in towns, but many still hunt in the traditional way. Some animal conservationists are demanding that these people give up their hunting rights.

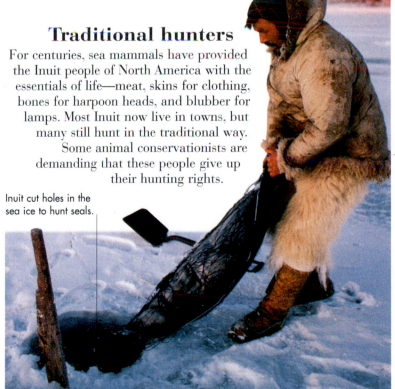

Inuit cut holes in the sea ice to hunt seals.

Costing the
EARTH

Much of the food on
sale today has been packed,
processed, or preserved, and shipped
halfway around the world. However, there's a high
environmental price to pay for all this food choice.
Processing and transporting food uses large
amounts of energy and creates problems such as
pollution and waste. What is more, fragile habitats
are being destroyed by small farmers trying to earn
a living by producing crops and livestock for export.

Hidden costs

Millions of burgers are eaten every
day, and each one has ingredients
from all over the world. For the
average US household, food
accounts for twice as much
greenhouse gas as driving,
and most of this comes
from farming, rather
than transporting
or packaging it.
Greenhouse gases from
fertilizers, cows, and
rice fields do as much
damage as carbon dioxide
from fuel burned
in farm machinery.

Lots of energy is
needed to process
bread and salad
dressing.

Beef is reared
cheaply in
developing
countries and
exported long
distances.

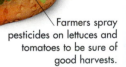

Farmers spray
pesticides on lettuces and
tomatoes to be sure of
good harvests.

Environmental destruction

Much of the beef for burgers eaten in the US is imported from Brazil.
Here, large areas of the Amazon rain forest have been cut down to
make way for cattle ranches. The thin soil can only support grazing for
a few years and the land quickly becomes bare, eroded, and ruined.

RIPENING BANANAS

You will need: 2 unripe bananas, 1 ripe banana, 2 polyethelene food bags, 2 bag ties.

3 LOOK AT THE bananas after two or three days. The unripe banana bagged with the ripe one will ripen faster than the unripe banana on its own.

1 PLACE ONE UNRIPE (green) banana in a bag along with the ripe one. Place the second unripe banana in a bag on its own.

2 SEAL BOTH BAGS with the ties. Leave the bananas on a sunny windowsill or in a warm place for a few days.

This shows that: ripening fruit gives off a gas—ethylene—which triggers fruit to ripen. The gas is used in warehouses to ripen fruit that has been picked "green" and chilled for export.

Storage and transportation

Supermarkets use vast amounts of electricity to run their lights, freezer cabinets, and cold storage. Great quantities of fuel are also needed for the ships, planes, and trucks that travel long distances to supply the stores; food transportation accounts for 11 percent of greenhouse gas emissions.

Food processing

Most of the fresh produce grown on farms is processed and packaged in factories before it ends up on the supermarket shelf. The production of ready-to-eat meals and long-life foods provides large numbers of people with jobs, but it makes food more expensive.

Recycling waste

Recycling is just one of the alternatives to burying garbage. Many cities are building recycling facilities, which reuse the packaging people throw away. If materials are recycled, fewer minerals need to be dug from the ground and fewer trees have to be cut down, which can only be good for the environment.

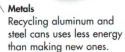

Glass Bottles and jars are melted down to make new glass products.

Plastics Manufacturers need to do more research into ways of recycling plastics.

Paper Recycling paper and cardboard saves trees and preserves forests.

Metals Recycling aluminum and steel cans uses less energy than making new ones.

Trash mountains

Tons of discarded food packaging and household waste are thrown away each week, and often end up buried in pits in the ground. This solution is not ideal, since the rotting waste can produce chemicals that pollute groundwater, or give off foul-smelling—and flammable—gases.

Glossary

acid rain rain in which harmful gases are dissolved, making it acidic

agroforestry growing crops and trees together to protect crops from the Sun

algae tiny organisms that live in water and provide food for fish and sea mammals

alien species animals that have been introduced artificially into a habitat that is not their own

atmosphere the wide, layered band of air above our Earth

battery farming farming in which animals, especially poultry, are kept in small, stacked cages

biotechnology the use of living cells, or molecules from cells, in industry or technology

breed to produce young

camouflage colors or patterns on an animal's body that allow it to blend into its surroundings

captivity a situation where animals are kept confined, such as in a zoo

clean energy energy produced without causing pollution

climate the average weather in a particular area over a long period of time

conservation the preservation and protection of natural resources

deforestation the act of clearing an area of forest

desalination taking the salt out of saltwater

drought a long period of time when there is no rain

ecology the relationship between living things and their environment

ecosystem in nature, a community and its environment that function as a self-contained unit

ecotourism tourism in unspoiled regions, managed to ensure that these regions remain unspoiled

endangered species a plant or animal species present in such small numbers that it is in danger of extinction

environment the natural world around us, including land, water, air, and living things

extinct no longer existing on Earth

factory farming *see* **intensive farming**

fertile refers to land that is full of plant nutrients

fertilizer a natural or chemical substance used to feed plants with nutrients

flotsam wreckage floating at sea

food chain a line of feeding links between different life-forms

forage to wander in search of food

fossil fuel fuel that is brought out of the earth and originates from the remains of living things

free range refers to food from animals that are allowed to wander around outside and eat whatever they choose

fungicide a chemical that is used to destroy fungi or limit their growth

genetic modification altering the genes of a plant or animal to change it, perhaps using genes from a completely different plant or animal

geothermal energy energy generated using heat from deep inside the Earth

global warming the gradual increase in average temperatures around the world

grassland land on which the dominant plants are grasses

greenhouse effect the process by which gases such as carbon dioxide trap the Sun's heat in the atmosphere

habitat the place, or type of place, where a plant or animal lives naturally

herbicide a chemical used to destroy or limit plant growth

hydroelectric power electricity generated from water

hydroponics growing crops in liquid, gravel, or sand with added nutrients instead of soil

hygiene conditions or practices that promote good health

insecticide a chemical used to kill insects or limit their growth

intensive farming farming carried out so that a large number of animals, or volume of crops, is produced in a limited space

intercropping growing one crop beside another to discourage pests, or to improve the soil's fertility

irrigate to supply land with water artificially, through a system of canals or channels

marine connected with the sea

microscopic something so small that it can only be seen through a microscope

monsoon a seasonal wind that brings heavy rainfall

nuclear energy energy created by changes in the nucleus of an atom

organic farming farming done without chemical fertilizers and pesticides

pesticide a chemical used to destroy insects and other crop pests

plankton the mass of tiny organisms

(phytoplankton) and animals (zooplankton) that float in the sea and provide food for sea creatures

pollution contamination by poisonous substances

polyps the tiny sea animals whose skeletons build up to form a coral reef

population the number of people in a town, city, or country

predator an animal that hunts, kills, and eats other animals

prey an animal that is hunted, killed, and eaten by a predator

radiation energy that travels as waves or particles—light, sunshine, and some forms of heat

recycle to reclaim or reuse something instead of throwing it away, or to process it into a useable product

rotation growing different crops, one after another, in one field

sewage human waste carried away by sewers

shanty town a collection of run-down dwellings

solar energy energy that comes from the Sun

sustainable able to be maintained at a fixed level without harming the environment

temperate moderate, not extreme—temperate regions are not too hot or too cold

threatened species a plant or animal that is at risk of becoming endangered

toxic describes something that causes harm, like a poison

tropical relating to the hot, humid regions around the equator

wetland tidal flat or swamp where the soil is permanently wet

Action Plan

If you care about the planet and want to help save its natural environment, there are many organizations that will help you to get involved. Here some useful addresses you can visit on the internet:

BBC Science and Nature
Information and events relating to science and the natural world. www.bbc.co.uk/science

BirdLife International
A leading bird conservation organization with branches worldwide. www.birdlife.org

Care for the Wild
A wildlife charity that protects animals from cruelty and exploitation. Based in the UK, but supports endangered species worldwide. www.careforthewild.org

Center for Marine Conservation
Runs programs and campaigns ranging from shark conservation to protection of coral reefs, and contains links to many other sites. www.cmc-ocean.org

Compassion in World Farming
An international organization that raises awareness about the suffering of farm animals. www.ciwf.co.uk

The Coral Reef Alliance
Promotes coral-reef conservation around the world. www.coral.org

Earthwatch Institute
An international organization that promotes conservation by funding education and expeditions, sometimes to remote parts of the world. www.earthwatch.org

Environmental Investigation Agency
An international campaigning organization committed to improving conservation laws—and making sure that existing laws are upheld. www.eia-international.org

European Association of Zoos and Aquaria
EAZA, dedicated to the welfare of captive animals, also monitors breeding programs all over Europe. www.eaza.net

Fauna and Flora International
An organization that conserves threatened species and ecosystems worldwide. www.fauna-flora.org

Food and Agriculture Organization of the United Nations
The UN agency that works to alleviate world poverty and hunger. www.fao.org

Friends of the Earth
An international network of environmental groups that commissions research and campaigns for changes in the law. www.foe.org

Global Action Plan
An independent charity committed to practical solutions for environmental and social problems. www.globalactionplan.org.uk

Greenpeace
One of the world's leading environmental organizations, involved in direct action to safeguard the planet's future. www.greenpeace.org

International Institute for Environment and Development
IIED is concerned with human welfare and the environment in poorer countries. www.iied.org

International Union for the Conservation of Nature and Natural Resources
IUCN is the world's largest conservation-related organization. www.iucn.org

Médecins Sans Frontières (Doctors Without Borders)
An international humanitarian organization that attempts to improve nutrition and health as well as providing medical assistance. www.msf.org

National Audubon Society (birds)
One of the US's foremost conservation organizations. www.audubon.org

Oceana
The largest international group dedicated to protecting and restoring the world's oceans. www.oceana.org

Oxfam
A development organization and relief agency working to put an end to world poverty and suffering. www.oxfam.org

People for the Ethical Treatment of Animals
PETA campaigns to prevent animal cruelty worldwide. www.peta-online.org

Project Seahorse
A program of extensive and diverse study and management of seahorses. www.projectseahorse.org

Rain forest Alliance
A US-based organization that supports rain-forest conservation. www.rainforest-alliance.org

Rain forest Concern
An organization that identifies and protects threatened areas of tropical rain forest. www.rainforest.org

Royal Society for the Protection of Birds
Europe's largest conservation charity, the RSPB helps to conserve wild birds in the UK, and elsewhere in the world. www.rspb.org.uk

Sea Shepherd Conservation Society
An organization that conserves and protects life in the oceans. www.seashepherd.org

Seaweb
News and information-based resource involving the ocean environment. www.seaweb.org

TRAFFIC International
Wildlife monitoring program that works to restrict the trade in live rare animals. www.traffic.org

United Nations Environment Program
UNEP was set up to safeguard and enhance the environment for future generations. www.unep.org

Whale and Dolphin Conservation Society
A charity that campaigns for the protection of whales, dolphins, and porpoises around the world. www.wdcs.org

World Conservation Monitoring Center
A unique website that gives visitors a chance to find out about the world's endangered animals. www.unep-wcmc.org

World Food Program of the United Nations
The food-aid organization of the UN, WFP helps to feed victims of disaster and works to improve nutrition for vulnerable people worldwide. www.wfp.org

Worldwide Fund for Nature
The WWF is the world's largest conservation organization. www.panda.org

Index

A
acid rain 23
air travel 9
algae 37, 41
alien species 56-57
Amazon River 10
Antarctica 50, 54
Arctic 16, 17, 54

B
Borneo 11
Brazil 11

C
clean energy 20-21, 22-23, 28-29
climate change 12, 14-15, 16-17, 18
coasts 42-43
conservation 54, 68-69, 70-71
coral reef 40-41, 55

D
deforestation 10-11
desalination 45
deserts 33, 55
disease 9, 17, 18,
drought 34-35

E
ecosystems 11
El Niño 19
endangered species 47, 56-57, 58-59, 60-61, 62-63, 64-65, 74

epiphytes 11
equator 10

F
famine 80-81
farming 18, 74-75, 76-77, 78-79
    livestock 86-87
    organic 75, 82-83
    fish 44, 45
    processing and transporting 90-91
fishing 88-89
floods 18-19
flowers 12
food chain 38
food production 74-75, 76-77, 78-79
    genetic modification 75, 84-85
forests 10-11
    forest fires 12-13
    temperate rain forest 10
    tropical rain forest 10
fossil fuels 14, 20-21, 22-23, 44

G
geothermal energy 29
global warming 14-15, 16-17, 19, 50-51, 54
grasslands 13, 55
greenhouse effect 14-15, 17, 50

H
habitats, endangered 54-55, 56-57, 58-59
Hong Kong 8

hunting animals
    for food 58-59
    for parts 60-61
    for pets 62-63
    for sport 64-65
hydroelectricity 29
hydroponics 35

I
insulation 28
irrigation 34, 35

L
litter 25, 42, 43
logging 11

N
New Orleans 18
nuclear energy 20, 25

O
oak trees 15
ocean life 38-39
ozone layer 23

P
parks and reserves 68-69
polar bear 16, 17
polar icecaps 25
pollution 9, 20-21, 24-25, 40, 41, 42, 43, 48-49
    air 22-23
    water 36-37
population 8-9
power generation 20-21

R
recycling 11, 27, 28, 91
Rio de Janeiro 9

S
sea
    levels 15, 50-51
    mining 44-45
    resources 44-45
seaweed 45
Siberia 12
solar power 28
sustainable timber 11

T
timber 10-11
tourism 41, 46-47, 54
trees 10-11, 12-13, 23

V
Venice 18

W
waste 26-27, 36-37, 42, 43, 48-49, 91
water 32-33, 34-35
water power see hydroelectricity
wetlands 33, 55
wind power 28

Z
zoos 70-71

Acknowledgments

Dorling Kindersley would like to thank: Katie Newman for design assistance; Fleur Star and Penny Smith for proofreading; and Rob Nunn for help with picture research.

Picture Credits
The publisher would like to thank the following for their kind permission to reproduce their photographs:

(key: a-above; b-below/bottom; c-center; f-far; l-left; r-right; t-top)

Alamy Images: Steve Bloom Images 2-3, 52-53; Doug Webb 18-19c. **K & K Ammann:** 58cr. **Ardea:** Hans D. Dossenbach 43bl; Kenneth W Fink 71br. **David Austen:** 20bl. **Mark Boulton:** 23ftl, 42-43. **John Cancalosi:** 29cb, 43cb, 55tl, 60-61. **Corbis:** Jason Hosking/zefa 30-31; Jiang Yi/Xinhua Press 80tr; Papa.graphics/Amanaimages 94tl; Boca Raton 91cl; David Reed 86bl; Roger Ressmeyer 77br; Reuters 22br; Jim Richardson 79tl; Guenter Rossenbach/zefa 94-95; Thierry Rousseau/Sygma 72-73; Paul Souders 6-7; Hans Strand 2tl; Kennan Ward 16-17b; Nevada Wier 35fcla; Michael S Yamashita 3tr. **Derek Croucher:** 42b. **Gerald Cubitt:** 11cr, 54bl, 57br. **Sue Cunningham Photographic:** 67tr. **DK Images:** Natural History Museum, London 4tl (green butterfly), 15cr (4 x butterflies). **John Downer:** 55br. **Alain Dragesco:** 64tl. **Ecoscene:** Andrew Brown 79ftr; Anthony Cooper 70-71; Hart 83br; Mike Whittle 83tl. **Ivor Edmonds:** 38fcr. **Eye Ubiquitous:** Bennett Dean 75cra. **Fauna & Flora International:** 11tr. **FLPA:** Holt 79br, 86-87, 91br; Holt Studios International/Julia Chalmers 86cb; Holt Studios International/Nigel Cattlin 35clb, 74cl, 82br; David Hosking 13br; Alwyn Roberts 87tr. **Getty Images:** 67cl; Odd Andersen/Afp 81tl; Sandra Baker 21cl; Adek Berry/Afp 81tr; Colorific!/Philippe Hays 51br;

Billy Hustace 28bc; Johnny Johnson 29fcla; John Lamb 8-9b; Frans Lanting 11tl; Paul McCormick 43fbr; Michael Melford 35br; Bryan Mullenix 32; Ben Osborne 37t; Popperfoto.com/Rafiqur Rahman 50-51; Ed Pritchard 9cb, 22tl; James Randhlev 55ca; Riser/Charles Krebs 15ftl; Michael Rosenfeld 91bl; Steve Shelton/Black Star 19crb; Stone/Jacques Jangoux 10-11b; Stone/Martien Mulder 4-5 (background); Keren Su 66bl; Taxi/Robert Jureit 10tl; Bob Torrez 49cr; Nick Vedros 26-27; Jeremy Walker 20-21; David Woodfall 36-37. **Greenpeace:** Hewetson 48-49. **Steve Hopkin:** 24fcrb. **Hutchison Library:** 68tl; Jeremy A Horner 74bc; Mary Jelliffe 33cla; Bernard Regent – DIAF 69tl. **Impact Photos:** Gerald Buthaud/Cosmos 12bc. **Julian Cotton Photo Library:** 8-9 (background), 14ca, 28t. **Steven C Kaufman:** 61cl, 65br. **David Kjaer:** 59b. **Kos Picture Source:** Gilles Martin-Raget 46-47. **C. Maddock:** 45cr. **Luiz Claudio Margo:** 61br. **Richard Matthews:** 67c. **Neil McAllister:** 41cla. **Joe McDonald:** 57tr. **Yva Momatik & John Eastcott:** 25tr. **naturepl.com:** Tom Walmsley 16tr. **NHPA/Photoshot:** Martin Harvey 57tl; Stephen Krasemann 16cl; Roy Waller 17c; David Woodfall 24-25 (background), 82tl; Norbert Wu 38clb. **Pacific Stock:** 65bl, 83bl. **Panos Pictures:** R. Berriedale-Johnson 46clb. **Doug Perrine:** 55tr. **Photofusion:** Environmental Images/Chris Martin 44tr; Environmental Images/David Sims 25clb; Environmental Images/Dominic Sansoni 29tc; Environmental Images/Images/Robert Brook 26cb, 37c; Environmental Images/Roger Grace 41tr; Environmental Images/Steve Morgan 15bl, 51tl. **Photolibrary:** Corbis 1; OSF/David M Dennis 59cl; OSF/Konrad Wothe 63bc; OSF/Mark Webster 40-41; OSF/Martyn Chillmaid 62br; OSF/Michael Fogden 15tr; OSF/Michael Pitts 48br; OSF/Richard Packwood 68-69; OSF/Rob Cousins 68br; OSF/

Stefan Meyers/Okapia 65tr; OSF/Steve Turner 69l; OSF/Tim Jackson 14br; OSF/Tony Martin 59tl. **David Ponton:** 14cra. **Dr. Eckart Pott:** 25tl. **Rex Features:** 79clb; Alexandra Boulant 27cla, 27tr; Christiana Laruffa 81br. **Robert Harding Picture Library:** 9br. **Brendan Ryan:** 64bl. **Centre for Science and Environment, India:** 35fbl. **Science Photo Library:** Martin Bond 75tc; Eye Of Science 17tc; Gene Feldman 38tr; R. B. Husar/NASA 18-19t; Chris Knapton 84-85; Jeff Lepore 12tl; Tom McHugh 23cla; Astrid & Hanns-Frieder Michler 38tl; Catherine Pouedras 20tl; Jerrican Weiss 23b. **Jonathan Scott:** 54c. **Still Pictures:** Kelvin Aitken 47c; B & C Alexander 89br; Adrian Arbib 18bl; Juan Carlos 89tr; Hanson Carroll 39cl; Nick Cobbing 85bc; Fred Dott 44-45; Mark Edwards 34tl, 76tl, 88tl, 89ca, 90l; Michael Gunther 57cr, 63tr; Robert Holmgren 84br; 85c; M & C Denis-Huot 13cr; John Paul Kay 74t; Marilyn Kazmers 41cr; Klein/Hubert 12br; John Maier 36clb; Gerard & Margi Moss 77c; Gil Moti 34bl; Knut Mueller/Das Fotoarchiv 80-81; Jim Olive 24cl; Edward Parker 89bl; Ray Pfortner 43fcr; Thomas Raupach 88b; Haratmut Schwarzbach 50tr, 81ca; Roland Seitre 47cr; Somboon-Unep 45tr; Joe St Leger 12-13 (background); Norbert Wu 55cl. **Kim Taylor:** 34-35 (background). **TopFoto.co.uk:** 20cr; UNEP/Daniel Frank 9tl. **Nigel Tucker:** 71cl. **Rod Williams:** 58bc. **Warren Williams:** 49tl. Norbert Wu: 48cb.

Jacket images: Front: iStockphoto.com: Jan Rysavy c (globe); Emrah Turudu cr (hand). **naturepl.com:** Aflo (background). **Back: Getty Images:** National Geographic /Taylor S. Kennedy tr. **Science Photo Library:** Martin Bond tl; Alexis Rosenfeld br; Daniel Sambraus bl. Spine: **iStockphoto.com:** Jan Rysavy ca (globe), cb (globe); Emrah Turudu ca (hand), cb (hand).

All other images © Dorling Kindersley
For further information see: www.dkimages.com